Professional
Grant Writer

"The Definitive Guide To Grant Writing Success."

" GO Where Others Have Stopped."

Lynne Marie Paeno

Testimonies

Lynne Paeno and her team are intelligent, creative and consistently receive rave reviews from all of my clients. Their writing capabilities, ability to engender diverse topics into cohesive ideas, and her ability to successfully manage all facets of the grant process elevates her to a level of success untouched by most.

Amy Wells
Seattle, Washington

I worked with their grant writers on two grants this past school year (2006-07). The quality of grant writing and level of service that they provided was incomparable. Lynne and her team were very knowledgeable about the educational grant process and helped us focus on those services that would most benefit our district. We were very pleased to have been awarded a large grant with their help. I look forward to working with Lynne and her team again in the future.

Debora Chan-Southwel
Risk Management Consultant
Lawndale Elementary School District

Testimonies

In addition to being an expert in the grant writing field, Lynne and her team are great communicators. Their friendly, personable and professional style makes clients feel at home, as they easily guide the client through the grant writing process (which for many has been a minefield experience). I thank her for the past successes on our behalf and look forward to working with her in the future.

Jack Hamilton, President
Good News Gifts, Inc.

Lynne and I have worked on several grant applications for Albuquerque Public Schools. I can honestly say that she takes the stress out of the grant writing process. She's both personable and professional. Lynne has made all the difference in our district grant awards.

Martha Fenstermacher
Albuquerque Public Schools

Lynne Paeno and her team stand out as the singularly most efficient, organized and fun writing group in my personal history. Their team makes proposal writing as easy as possible for the customer.

Michele Hobza
Sacramento City Unified School District

Grant Writers Institute

Grant Writers Institute LLC (GWI) was founded with the vision of helping individuals, foundations and government organizations to more efficiently and successfully receive grant funding for projects. GWI understands how difficult grant proposals can be, and knows that not every person completely understands how the process works With the help of GWI many organizations are able to not only reduce their cost of writing the grant proposal, but historically the grant writers have been able to produce a 70% success rate in receiving grant funding.   The knowledge and experience that GWI has allows companies to truly be able to outsource their grant proposal to individuals who write grant proposals every day.

For more information contact GWI at

1-877-296-9387 or go to www.grantwritersinstitute.org

Professional Grant Writer

"The Definitive Guide to Grant Writing Success"

Lynne Marie Paeno

LANDMARK PUBLISHING GROUP

KANSAS CITY, MO.

Landmark Publishing Group

Copyright© 2008

Landmark Publishing Group books may be ordered through booksellers or by contacting:

Landmark Publishing Group
PO Box 445
Paola, Kansas 66071
www.landmarkpublishinggroup.com

Cover Design by Binary Catalyst

Printed in the United States of America

A large thanks to: Landmark Publishing, ASI, and Binary Catalyst for making this book possible. Special thanks to ASI Management for their support and encouragement and to Meggie Chapman for her invaluable contributions and expertise. My wish is that this book offers life changing knowledge to each and every reader. Thank you to everyone who made this book possible.

-Lynne Paeno-

TABLE OF CONTENTS

1

Introduction

Let's be honest. Finding and writing grants can be an intimidating prospect. Whether you are looking at a 1-page local foundation proposal or a 60-page grant guidance package from the federal government, as you glaze over the instructions, processing terms like 'needs statement,' 'eligibility requirements,' 'electronic submission' and 'SPOC compliance,' you most likely are feeling defeated before you begin.

Grant writing does not have to be overwhelming. By following this step-by-step approach, you will be able to implement a proven process that you can duplicate for every grant application, as well as come to better understand grant writing requirements and terms and ultimately pad your fund balance! Just remember that step-by-step does not mean that it will not require work and planning on your part, but the rewards will be well worth the effort.

The information in each chapter of this guide is based on both tried and proven--and failed--practices from experts in the field and my own experiences as a professional grant writer for more than 10 years. After writing funding proposals for others as a freelancer and for my own organization as an Executive Director of a non-profit agency, I fine-tuned a strategy that I use every time I write a grant. It truly helps keep me and my team of grant writers on track and ensures that important pieces and steps of the proposal process are fully addressed.

When I launched my own company in 2003, I felt certain I had been through it all – I had lots of success in securing funding for clients around the country AND my fair share of disappointments for projects that were not funded. We all have our horror stories – here is mine: I submitted a large federal grant electronically only to learn it was rejected by the funder because it was a few lines of text over the page limit! Chalk that one up to 'lessons learned' – you can bet that never happened again. Page length and format went straight into my checklist of items to be triple checked before submitting an application.

Even though our team has written or assisted in the development of over $80 million in grant awards, there is never a guarantee your grant will be funded, no matter how well it is constructed and thought out. So, I'm compelled to advise you to not take rejection personally and not to give up if your first or even second application is not funded. As you become more versed in the process you will see your success rate increase and your confidence will soar. There is a lesson to be learned from both success and rejection. It is the savvy grant writer who knows how to recognize how to turn those lessons learned into fine-tuning their craft.

The cadre of writers on my team follows this standard approach in writing grants for each of our clients, whether it is the first grant for the organization/individual, or the fiftieth. Every project and client receives the same level of attentive service and attention to detail, and every proposal is equally important whether it is a local request for $100 for supplies or $1 million for a school project.

Are we successful? I measure success not only by the funds received for my clients -- although I am sure they would put that at the top of their list -- but also, by ensuring the money they invest in grant writing services is well spent. They learn enough about the process as we work together to ultimately be able to work independently to earn their own successes.

What You Will Find in this Book

      This comprehensive guide will give you answers and simple examples to some not-so-simple questions: Where do we look for funding? How do we apply for grants? Do we qualify? Do we have the time to figure this all out? Should we just hire a professional? In each chapter, you will find answers to these questions and more, covering the essentials from planning, searching for grants and the development of proposals, to submitting your proposal and what to do and expect after you submit your application to the funder. Each section discussed will offer tips, resources and even templates and samples to help you in the process of grant writing. Remember grant money is just a proposal away.

Good luck!

Chapter 1

Establishing Funding Goals

Establishing funding goals requires some planning on your part. I wish I could tell you that you do not have to do some back-end work to get ready to start applying for grants, but as you will see as we progress throughout each chapter, the planning you do in the beginning will be useful to you in both determining what types of funders will be right for you *and* as you write your application response. Appropriate planning will help you transform your ideas into competitive projects -- competitive meaning a better probability of being funded – and that is the whole idea, right?

Establishing your funding goals can be accomplished in just four steps: 1) who you are; 2) what you do; 3) what you need; and 4) where you want to go.

Step 1 – Who you are

Each funder selects the types of organizations/individuals they want to support. Some common 'types' of organizations include:

- 501 C 3 non-profit organizations

- Educational institutions (e.g. elementary and secondary independent schools or districts, post-secondary institutions, institutes of higher education)

- Government agencies

- Federally recognized tribes

- Minority- or women owned-businesses or corporations (MWBEs)

- Private businesses or corporations

Step 2 – What you do

What you do is your organization/individual mission and services – its purpose. If you do not have a formal mission statement, take a look at the services you provide or the type of products you offer.

For example: ABC Agency is a 501 C 3 non-profit Homeless Shelter *(who you are)* whose mission is to foster public awareness in the community about the homeless population, provide life-changing services to the homeless population including job training, job placement, housing assistance and personal counseling *(what you do)*.

Step 3 - What you need

Most funders will say you should base your proposal on real need, <u>not</u> just on an idea, even if it is a really creative idea. Use this process as an opportunity to ask yourself and discuss your needs with your team using the following questions:

- ♣ Are there gaps and/or weaknesses in current programs or services that need to be addressed? What are they?

- ♣ Are donations decreasing? Why?

- ♣ Is funding needed for everyday expenses (operational support) to sustain programs or services?

- ♣ Is there technology or equipment needed to improve programs or services?

- ♣ Is there a need to build capacity in your organization to expand it or make it more efficient/effective? (Capacity building is a common grant term that refers to the development of financial, technical or human resources).

- ♣ Is there a specific demand or need for services in the community that needs to be addressed?

- ♣ Is there a special project, innovative or model program needed that will meet a local, state or national need?

- ♣ Is there a need to acquire or improve a major physical asset, like remodeling a building or purchasing a van?

Most likely you will identify multiple needs. Take this list and prioritize from highest to lowest. You can determine your priorities by asking the following questions: What do we need *now*? For example, if we do not have 'blank' we will be forced to close our doors. Which identified priorities will have the greatest impact on our organization/individual and community needs? Do we have the current staff and resources to implement if we receive funding tomorrow? Prioritizing your needs is an important step as it sets the direction for your funding strategy that we will address in the next chapter.

For example: ABC Agency has put funding for their job training and referral center as a highest priority because they have less than six months' worth of funds available to continue the programming and donations from community businesses and individuals are down from last year due to a loss of major businesses in the community. If ABC Agency does not receive funding for staffing and programming for their referral center soon, they will have to close the program down after six months.

Step 4 – Where you want to go

Once your needs have been prioritized, use these priorities to determine your funding goals *(where you want to go)*. Your funding goals are essentially what you plan to do with the support or funds raised. Goals should be broad; you will go into greater detail during the development of your proposal.

Questions to assist you in determining your goals:

- ♣ What will this project accomplish?

- ♣ What is the overall purpose?

- ♣ What are the anticipated results of the project?

- ♣ How will grant funding benefit my organization or individual business services or programs?

For example: Grant funding for this project will provide training for sixth- to twelfth-grade teachers across the nation to study ocean curricula and learn how to integrate these essential subjects into their classroom curriculum substantially improving the ocean literacy of teachers and students across the country.

Align your funding goals with your organization/individual's mission

It is imperative to align your funding goals with your mission. How will funding goals affect your future? Ask yourself honestly if the goals are in line with your mission or purpose, or are you just applying for the funds because they are available? If a project falls outside of your mission, extensive justification will be necessary to persuade a funder to fund your application. When your mission is reflected in your funding goals, it presents a strong and buyable rationale to a funder. A good example would be if you are a non-profit food bank and your mission is to feed the disadvantaged people of your community and your goal is to develop a community garden.

Putting the pieces together

Once you put these steps together -- who you are, what you do, what you need and where you want to go, it is a good idea to write them out and keep them on hand so you can refer to them frequently throughout the grant seeking and writing process. It does not need to be complex. *Just the facts, ma'am!*

A sample narrative statement of your funding goals and a sample chart are listed below:

You are a non-profit organization *(who you are)* that operates an after-school program for at-risk students *(what you do)* that has been turning students away consistently for over a year because you are low on staff, cramped on space and have minimal supplies *(what you need)*. Your goal would be to secure funding to expand your after-school program *(where you want to go)* by finding and transferring to a larger space *(Priority 1)*, hiring additional staff *(Priority 2)* and purchasing additional supplies *(Priority 3)* which furthers your mission to serve academically at-risk students to increase academic achievement and increase prosocial behaviors through a safe after-school environment.

Who You are	What you Do	What you Need	Where you Want to Go	Funding Priorities
Non-profit educational	Provide after school programs for academically at-risk students	Staff, space and supplies	Expand after school program to accommodate additional students	1. Space relocation 2. Hire additional staff 3. Purchase additional supplies

Congratulations on completing your funding goals! The funding goals you have just developed and prioritized are the basis for your entire grant seeking and writing experience.

Chapter 2

Developing A Funding Strategy

Now that you have developed your funding goals, you are thinking, "*show me the money,*" right? Well almost...just one more test of patience—creating a funding strategy or funding plan. If you only plan to apply for one grant and you've already identified the project, you could skip this process and jump ahead to Chapter 3. However, if you truly want to impress your board, staff or boss, putting a little thought into a well thought out and researched funding plan for the next one to two years will do the trick. A funding strategy is simply a list of grant opportunities aligned with each of your funding goals that gives you a quick snapshot of the grants available with a timeline of due dates to help you manage and plan your work for the year.

ABC Agency Funding Strategy			1/1/20__ to 12/30/20__	
Funding Goal 1: *Your funding goal or priorities – where you want to go.*				
Shortlist: *yes, no, maybe*	**Funding Opportunity:** *title and priority*	**Type of Support:** *source of grant and type of assistance*	**Details:** *eligibility, how to apply, contact info*	**Timeline:** *key dates*
Funding Goal 2: *Your funding goal or priorities – where you want to go.*				
Shortlist: *yes, no, maybe*	**Funding Opportunity:** *title and priority*	**Type of Support:** *source of grant and type of assistance*	**Details:** *eligibility, how to apply, contact info*	**Timeline:** *key dates*

16

You are already able to fill in your funding goals and priorities from what you learned in Chapter 1; this chapter will help you fill in the rest of the information.

Screening – The search is on

Screening is a four-pronged process which helps you determine who you will approach for support: 1) understanding who provides grants; 2) clarify the type of assistance you are looking for; 3) determine the categories of funding you will seek; and 4) identifying current and forecasted funding opportunities.

Who provides grants?

There are five main types of granting organizations: federal government agencies, state government agencies, local government agencies (i.e. county, city and community), foundations and corporations.

Funding trends

Federal government provides over 400 billion dollars in funding through 26 federal grant making agencies and over 1,000 grant programs. These grants are distributed for a variety of purposes, including to: stimulate the economy, distribute tax revenue, provide equal opportunities, protect national security, and to support special interest and groups. All kinds of organizations (tribal, non-profit, religious, and educational, etc.) are eligible to pursue a number of grant programs from federal government agencies.

Charitable giving hit a record high in 2006 at $295 billion. Charitable giving includes foundation grants, corporate and corporate foundation giving, individual donations and charitable bequests. Foundation grants and corporate giving accounted for nearly $50 billion of the 2006 total. About one-third of the total 2006 donations went to religious organizations, about $97 billion. Education grants represented the second largest sector, with 14 percent of the total or $41 billion. Other key giving areas included health, arts and culture, the environment and animals and international affairs. About $3.5 billion in gifts was the estimated fair-market value of donated medical supplies and medicines.

Foundations are in business to give money away and corporations often donate a small percentage of their profits to support their interests and priorities. In general, foundations and corporations will provide support to non-profit organizations and educational institutions, but check eligibility guidelines for individual requirements.

Funding cycles

Foundations review applications quarterly and some have rolling deadlines (ongoing throughout the year). A majority of state and federal grants are announced in late fall through spring. Typically applicants for government grants are given 30 or more days to prepare applications. Announcements of funding awards for both will vary; however, guidelines will usually specify a response period. The key for both is to keep in contact with funder contacts for all phases of the process.

You can learn more about specific funding trends and cycles through Internet research, by reviewing previous award listings posted on grant agency websites, or by researching Internal Revenue Service 990 Forms, which indicate how charitable dollars have been spent in a tax year.

What types of assistance are we looking for?

Each funding source provides different kinds of assistance across a variety of categories. Yes, we are interested in grant money awards, but you may want to consider if you are interested in other types of support. Alternatives to money awards include:

- *In-kind contributions* are donations of equipment, supplies, space or services. An organization may allow you to use their offices for a Saturday clinic or a company may donate their old computer equipment.

- *Volunteer hours* are the contribution of staff time. This could be a legal firm offering to provide free attorney hours to assist you with legal matters.

18

♣ *Scholarships,* most commonly for educational purposes, are gifted aid that does not have to be repaid.

♣ *Corporate sponsorships* provide a way for a company to market their product or service through a mutually beneficial agreement. An example of this growing trend in giving would be a company paying for the production of learning materials in exchange to put their name and logo on the cover of each binder.

♣ *Direct Loans* are financial assistance provided through the lending of federal monies for a specific period of time, with a reasonable expectation of repayment. Such loans may or may not require the payment of interest. College tuition loans would be an example of direct loans.

♣ *Guaranteed/Insured Loans* are programs in which the federal government makes an arrangement to indemnify a lender against part or all of any defaults by those responsible for repayment of loans. These are often small business loans provided by the Small Business Administration or first home buyer mortgage programs.

What category of support do you require?

Detail of each funding opportunity is provided in the grantmaker's guidelines. The guidelines will describe what grants the funder offers and the categories of support they will provide. Use the following outline of typical categories of funding to identify what type of support you will seek to achieve your funding goals; make sure you insert the data in your chart. You will approach funders whose guidelines indicate these areas of interest. Your goals may match multiple areas of support:

General operating support, sometimes called unrestricted support, covers the day-to-day costs of running your organization or business. Office space, staff salaries, marketing materials and other essentials are all considered general operating support. General operating support may be harder to secure; most funders want a beginning and an end to a project so they can determine effectiveness and impact.

Capital project funding is for the specific purpose of building a building, undertaking a major building renovation or expansion, or purchasing a major piece of necessary equipment. For example, the city's fire department needs a new fire truck with modernized equipment, an extraordinary capital expense that is most likely not in the city's strapped budget.

An *endowment campaign* is a fund-raising campaign that raises money for an organization to invest rather than spend. The monies raised are placed in an endowment fund, which provides a permanent, continuous stream of funds from interest earned to be used for operating support, cover capital expenditures, or fund special projects and programs.

Equipment funding is for costly supplies, materials, tools and smaller machinery and furniture purchases. Athletic gear, office furniture, computers and printers, and medical machinery would all fall under equipment funding. Let's say your community center needs to purchase a portable automated external defibrillator (AED) to better prepare for a medical emergency. This would be considered an equipment purchase.

Capacity building funds are used to strengthen and bolster sustainability and/or enable expansion. There are five critical areas of capacity building: 1) leadership development, 2) organizational development, 3) program development, 4) revenue development strategies, and 5) community engagement.

Project-based support is by far the most common form of funding and is used specifically to launch a program or support a project. This could mean funding for an innovative new program or service or a project that will address gaps and weaknesses in your services, impact your community and/or serve as a model program that can be replicated around the country.

Formula grants are allocations of money to states or their subdivisions in accordance with a distribution formula.

What funding opportunities are out there and how do I find them?

So, now that you have an idea of who provides grants and what types of support you are looking for, you are ready for the next step – the screening process, or searching for available funding opportunities. Every day there are more and more resources available to search for grants. You will have to be resourceful in your search methods. If you choose not to hire a consultant or to not pay for access to a database or newsletter of grant resources, you can wade through newspapers, subscribe to free newsletters, monitor business and annual reports, join online discussion groups, call local corporations and foundations, network and gather intelligence through personal and professional connections, but by far the most useful tool to perform searches will be the Internet. This is the quickest and most comprehensive way to find grants.

Surfing the net

Allow yourself plenty of time for Internet research. You definitely will not find everything in one place. As you find sites that are useful to you, remember to add them to your web page 'favorites' or write them down. This will save you time and allow you to return to them frequently.

General grant seeking

Novice grant seekers may want to start out by performing a full Internet search to find grants and grant databases. This will give you an understanding of the infinite sources at your disposal. To do this you will use your general search engine and type in grants + any number of key words. For example, if I am looking for grant databases, I would type in: grants + database or: grants + search. If I am looking for education grants, I would type in: grants + database + education or: grants + search + education. To do a specific search for grants that will fund K-12 reading intervention software, I would type in: education + grants +

21

reading intervention + software. You may have to mix up your key words or omit specific language, but you will surely turn up pages and pages of results. Several free grant databases will surface through these general searches. Snoop around different grant databases to see which are most maneuverable, which ones are current and which ones have the most available data that applies to you.

Other useful leads may also be returned from your searches. Links will often turn up that include the names of agencies that were awarded the type of grant(s) you are looking for. Perhaps you are searching for grants + community policing support and your search turns up ABC College received a Community Oriented Policing Services (COPS) grant from the U.S. Department of Justice. In this case, jot down the funding agency name so you can look them up to see if they are still offering the same grant or something similar. Remember, be resourceful.

Federal government grant seeking

Federal government agencies post grants on Grants.gov (www.grants.gov), a portal for publicizing grant announcements and electronic applications (discussed in Chapter 7). This portal allows you to perform simple and advanced searches for all discretionary grants offered by the 26 Federal grant-making agencies. Discretionary grants are competitive and awards are based on a review process that determines which applications best meet the requirements. Through Grants.gov you can also sign up for electronic notification and receive all new grant announcements or select notifications based on specific criteria such as funding category, eligibility or funding agency. Considerably more time consuming is to go to each individual federal agency to see their current grant postings, unless you have a specific target – U.S. Department of Education for education grants. Other resources are posted in the Federal Register (http://fr.cos.com/cgi-bin/search), a daily publication of grant notices, legal announcements, etc. or the Catalog of Federal Domestic Assistance (http://12.46.245.173/cfda/cfda.html), which offers a searchable listing of federal grant opportunities, but Grants.gov offers the most current data and quickest access.

State government grant seeking

State funding opportunities are listed on your state's web page and searchable by department or through a basic web search. If I am an independent filmmaker in Arizona and I am looking for a grant to produce a documentary, I would do a basic search through the Arizona State Government website search engine for 'art grants' or similar key words. This would turn up responses to investigate further. Or, if I knew there was the Arizona Commission on the Arts, I might go directly to their web page and look at current or forecasted (upcoming) funding opportunities. School Grants (www.schoolgrants.org) is a great resource site for opportunities available through State Departments of Education and other State agencies.

Local government grant seeking

Local grants are listed on county, city or community websites, but these grants are less publicized and harder to find. It may take calling your respective local agency to gain information about opportunities.

Foundation and corporate grant seeking

Foundation and corporate grants are posted in myriad locations. You can use the general search engine method described earlier in this chapter, you can go directly to various foundation or corporation websites and search for their philanthropy/giving page, or you can search several foundation and corporate giving databases.

To use a general search engine you can type in: foundation + grants + a variety of keywords related to your goals. For example, you need to find funding to help purchase a new community center building, so I would type in: foundation + grants + capital. Or I could type in: foundation + grants + capital + community center. I might even add my geographic location for funders who grant specifically in my community. This brings up several foundations and their links to investigate further.

23

You can also search for foundations nationally or by community at Foundations On-Line (www.foundations.org).

Many grantseekers will go directly to high profile, large or well performing foundation or corporation websites and explore their respective giving guidelines. A nifty trick for familiarizing yourself with large corporations that often have large philanthropy budgets is to get the Fortune 100 or 500 list and start looking at each company's respective philanthropy trends and available grants.

Philanthropic databases will allow you to hone in specifically on foundation and corporate giving. Most of the major databases are free for searching by foundation/corporation name; however, if we had this information, we would go directly to the funder's website. These major databases that identify funders by type, category, etc., usually will charge a service fee. Search the Internet to find free searchable databases or more often databases that post listings of current open opportunities. Sometimes these resources will even sort by support category or geographic giving location or type. For example, The Foundation Center (http://lnp.fdncenter.org/finder.html) allows you to search online for free by name, city, state or zip and EIN number. Do not worry -- searching for opportunities get easier as you get more familiar with the available resources.

Short-listing – is this grant a good fit or not?

During your searches track the different funding opportunities in your chart that you feel may be appropriate to approach for support based on the type of organizations/individuals they fund *(who you are)* and the types of projects they fund *(match to what you do)*. This list will be used to determine your eligibility and competitiveness of an opportunity through more in-depth research or short-listing.

Determining eligibility

Short-listing can be done by sending off for eligibility criteria by mail or email, reading eligibility guidelines on funder websites, or over the telephone. Eligibility is determined by researching what the funder's requirements are: re-verify they offer the type of grant you are seeking and that you are eligible for their grants determine if their priorities are aligned with yours; and check if they serve your geographic location. This is done by reviewing the grantmaker's guidelines or request for proposals. Grantmaker guidelines will indicate a target market or type of project for which the funder is willing to provide support and how to initially approach them, as well as previously awarded projects. A Request for proposal (RFP), sometimes referred to as request for application (RFA), is an invitation to submit applications or proposals for specific programs. In short, the RFP lists project specifications and application procedures. Usually an RFP will have an overview section which will provide you with information to determine your eligibility. Use the RFP or guidelines to determine if the opportunity is a good fit. If it is, mark or highlight the grant on your chart. If it is not, you can cross it off. If it is a 'maybe,' mark it in a different way for further research.

Second-hand Research

Databases and resource sites may provide guidelines and information regarding grant application procedures for multiple funders. However, even though one-stop shopping is a huge timesaver, do not rely on any data except for the data provided by the grantmaker. Purchasing a CD of well-researched resources is another option. Check that the product has been recently updated before you purchase. This method gives you a pretty thorough list of funders in one place that you can use to further research for details via the Internet or by calling the funder directly. Prices vary for these kinds of products, but are well worth the price if they can save you time.

Although the information available second-hand may be accurate, taking the time to write to or call the grantmaker or going directly to their website makes much more sense than preparing an application that will not even be considered. Funders often comment that it is amazing how many applications are submitted that do not meet the basic eligibility criteria and are therefore disqualified from even being reviewed.

Contacting the funder directly

I strongly suggest contacting the funder either by telephone or email to introduce yourself and to share (briefly) what your project entails. Getting feedback from the funder accomplishes three important things: 1) ensures that you do not waste time writing a proposal they may not be interested in; 2) helps you learn straight from the horse's mouth what types of programs the funder IS interested in, especially if your project is not a good fit or their priorities are vague; and 3) sets up a recall relationship with the funder – they will remember your call when they review your application. Program officers are government agency officers in charge of a grant program. Most program officers welcome phone calls and emails. This contact can prove to be extremely insightful and begins a relationship building process that is instrumental for a partnership. They do not want you to waste your time as much as they do not want to spend time reviewing something that is not aligned with their mission or agenda. So do your research before submitting!

Determine competitiveness and capacity

Once you have determined that your agency type and funding priority meets the funder's eligibility requirements, use the data you have documented in your Funding Strategies chart to analyze each opportunity. Which opportunities do we have the best shot at? Which guidelines do our goals seem to align with best? Be sure to take application deadlines into consideration. Are there overlapping deadlines? Do we have the time and resources to develop multiple applications at once? Be realistic about the time required to complete each grant application and finalize your shortlist based on what you can realistically accomplish. An application's quality will suffer significantly if you rush an application or are trying to complete more than one application for the same deadline period. If you determine that you want to submit more than one or several applications and realize you cannot handle the workload yourself, think about hiring a professional grant writer to help.

Establish a timeline

Your timeline will consist of important application dates and deadlines for your final shortlist of grants. Specifically, the RFP, application or competition announcement date, the time/dates you are allotting to the application preparation process, the submission deadline, a date for possible submission follow-up, an estimated award date and, if available, intended project start date. The world of grants can be very fickle and it should be noted that grant deadlines can change at any time. For example, the U.S. Department of Education posts forecasted dates (http://www.ed.gov/fund/grant/find/edlite-forecast.html) for when they plan to announce a competition, but keep in mind that these projected dates are not set in stone, so watch for the actual announcement of the grant or call the program officer for more information. Grantmakers also often extend proposal deadline dates, so again, watch closely for these changes and you can always add in an opportunity to your funding strategy at a later time that you originally eliminated because of overlapping due dates.

If you are serious about ongoing grant writing, continuously monitor and revise your funding strategy based on any new or forecasted grants that are better aligned with your priorities or immediate needs.

Final Funding Strategy

If you decided to use a chart and you have been filling it in to create your final funding strategy, it will most likely look something like this:

ABC Agency Funding Strategy   1/1/20__ to 12/30/20__

Funding Goal 1: *To provide a research-based reading intervention program to improve reading levels of students in grades K-3.*

Support Category: *Project-based support*

Shortlist: *yes, no, maybe*	Funding Opportunity: *title and priority*	Type of Support: *source of grant and type of assistance*	Details: *eligibility, how to apply, contact info*	Timeline: *key dates*
Yes	Youth Literacy Grant - Grants provide funding to help with the implementation or expansion of literacy programs for students who are below grade level or experiencing difficulty reading.	Dollar General Cash Award	Schools, public libraries, nonprofit organization Download application online. Contact: XXX	Deadline: 4/17/20__ Project Start Date: 8/1/20__

| Maybe | Improving Literacy through School Libraries – Helps LEAs improve reading achievement by providing students with increased access to up-to-date school library materials; well-equipped, technologically advanced school library media centers; and professionally certified school library media specialists. | USDOE Cash Award | Local education agencies (LEAs) in which at least 20 percent of students served are from families with incomes below the poverty line may apply. Submit full proposal via Grants.gov Contact: XXX | Deadline: 6/30/20__ Project Start Date: 3/10/20__ |
| No | Toyota Family Literacy Program – | Toyota and the National Center | Emphasis on primary and secondary schooling. In addition to funding national programs, Toyota supports | Deadline: 6/30/20__ |

To help parents in at-risk Hispanic and other immigrant families improve their English, education, work and parenting skills, while helping their children succeed in school.	for Family Literacy (NCFL) Cash Award	the social well-being of communities where it has major operations Toyota Online Application Contact: XXX	Project Start Date: 9/1/20__

Funding Goal 2: *To renovate the ABC high school's gym to meet building safety codes providing a safe gathering area and activity center for students and the community.*

Support Category: *Capital project*

Shortlist: *yes, no, maybe*	Funding Opportunity: *title and priority*	Type of Support: *source of grant and type of assistance*	Details: *eligibility, how to apply, contact info*	Timeline: *key dates*
Yes	Foundation Grant Program	DEFG Charitable Trust	Non-profit organizations and educational institutions.	Deadline: 2/15/20__

	Unrestricted	Cash award	Submit full proposal to: XXXXXX Contact: XXX	Project Start Date: 4/1/20__
Maybe	Capital Grant Program New vehicles or equipment, equipment replacement and modernizatio n, improvement s to facilities, and educational materials.	ABC Foundati on Cash award with match	Non-profit public charities. Online application. Contact: XXX	Deadline: 6/30/20__ Project Start Date: 9/1/20__
No	Discretionary Construction Grant Program For emergency repairs and modernization	USDOE Cash award	In general, to be eligible to apply for an emergency construction grant, an LEA must: 1) Enroll a high proportion (at least 40 percent) of federally connected children in average daily attendance (ADA) who reside on Indian lands or who reside on	Deadline: 6/30/20__ Project Start Date: 9/1/20__

of school facilities		Federal property and have a parent on active duty in the U.S. uniformed services; 2) Have a school that enrolls a high proportion of one of these types of students; or 3) Be eligible for funding for heavily impacted LEAs under section 8003(b)(2). Full proposal via Grants.gov Contact: XXX	

Since your funding goals may have more than one funding opportunity, choose the grant you will pursue first. Review your need and funding goal so it is fresh in your mind because it is now time to move past the pre-planning and researching phase and get ready to tackle your first application. The next two chapters will take you through gathering the information you need to write your application, and the actual process of writing a competitive grant proposal.

Chapter 3

Gathering What you Need to Write

You are now armed and dangerous with your funding strategy and have chosen your first funding opportunity. It is now time to gather the information you will need to begin putting your grant application together. This process, sometimes referred to as 'housekeeping,' includes: obtaining data and other background material, reading through the RFP or grant guidelines, developing a proposal outline based on the RFP/grant criteria and identifying any other staff or business members who will play a role in developing the proposal and conceptualizing the project.

Compiling data

As a grant writer you will need to tell your organization or individual story and sell a conceivable program for each and every grant proposal. It is extremely hard to create a proposal from thin air. You must have plenty of data to draw from. So, you gather data. Begin by collecting the following information – most of this information most likely already exists in the form of publications, brochures, or a website; otherwise, a little research on your part is in order:

- ♣ General description of your organization and its mission, or a profile statement. A profile statement is boiler plate information about you, your organization, and its community, including where it is located; history; successes; and specific target audience or customers. It may include statistics, demographics, anecdotes, etc.

- ♣ An annual report or continuous improvement plan.

- ♣ Demographic and socioeconomic data on your community. This can be found online through the U.S. Census Bureau, City-data.com, Epodunk.com or Wikipedia.org.

- ♣ Any previous grants previously written, funded or not.

- ♣ Previous evaluation reports for your project, program or services.

34

♣ Research reports that may be related to your field, project, program or services, and research that substantiates your identified need and supports your proposed solution/goals.

♣ Newspaper clippings that support the need for your project or demonstrate program or individual recognition.

♣ Resumes for organization/individual leadership and any personnel who will be involved in the grant project.

♣ School and district report cards, if applicable.

♣ Letter of 501 (c) 3 or other proof of tax-exempt status. If you are a non-profit with tax-exempt status, almost every grantmaker will ask you to include this with your proposal.

♣ Be sure you know your organization/individual's Tax ID Number or Employer Identification Number and your Data Universal Numbering System number (DUNS). Dun & Bradstreet assigns the DUNS number and is now required for all government applications and can take at least 24 hours to obtain. We suggest you call to obtain a DUNS number vs. emailing or writing for one.

You may not have all of the items listed above and may have to do some additional research for what you do not already have. Pull the items you do have together prior to the development process. You will not want to deal with the logistics and added stress of trying to track down needed statistics or facts while you are focusing on writing a proposal. Also, make sure you have a general idea of what is in each of these documents so you can refer to them more quickly to extract information. Sometimes we refer to these items as our pot of gold. So many times have we gone through these materials and found facts, figures or other information that pull the proposal together or really create that slam dunk factor (competitive edge).

Gather intelligence

We also strongly suggest you learn about the funder you are applying to. Take notes on the similarities of the funder's mission and yours, and then link those similarities together in your proposal. Look for key terminology and language used by the funder to weave into your application. Funders will appreciate your interest in their organization, philanthropy efforts and services. It also indicates you are not just sending a template proposal to a gazillion different funders hoping to get lucky.

Decoding the request for proposal (RFP) or grant guidelines

READ through the RFP or grant guidelines. Yes, they are boring and usually quite lengthy, but the information obtained is critical to successful grant writing. Pay particular attention to:

The Cover Letter of the Application Package - This overview includes such information as program purpose, applicable rules, the contact person's name, phone number and e-mail address, and sources of additional information.

Purpose of the Program - Being clear about the purpose of the program will help you respond in a focused way to the priorities and requirements, not just to your needs.

Submission Deadline – The date and time the application must be submitted. For applications sent in by mail (paper applications), check to see if the due date posted in the guidance is the *mailing* (postmark) date or the *date of receipt*. No matter how you submit, paper or electronic, late applications are not accepted, and waivers for individual exceptions are not granted.

Amount of Funding and Number of Awards - The number of awards projected indicates how competitive the process will be. You may choose not to apply when there are fewer than ten. Or you may decide your program has that slam dunk factor and has a good chance of being one of a handful funded.

Estimated Range of Awards – Your proposal's requested budget must be within the estimated range. This financial information will help you conceptualize the scope of your request. If the grant is for a maximum of $25,000, you would not plan to purchase a building – maybe furniture.

Length of Awards - Multi-year awards require a multi-year project design, objectives, and budget. You also have to plan to fully administer and expend the grant funds for your project within the funding period. Some projects have a 1-year budget, others 18 months or multi-year; so keep this in mind when planning your budget and activities. If you have questions, always contact the program officer and ask for clarification.

Application Transmittal Instructions – This is how you submit your proposal. Be sure you understand the submission instructions and submission systems for transmitting your proposals. Electronic systems may require advanced registration, which will be indicated in this section as well. Allow plenty of time to register for any electronic submission systems. Grants.gov can take several days for registration and www.Grantsolutions.gov (Health and Human Services) can be accomplished in just minutes. Navigate through the system prior to submission day; be familiar with how things work. Most online systems are user-friendly and offer a tutorial that walks you through each function.

Authorizing Statute – More common in government grants, this often contains the rationale behind the legislation authorizing the grant competition, as well as other useful information.

Intergovernmental Review Single Point of Contact (SPOC) – This section will indicate if there are any requirements for your state's SPOC. Each state can designate an entity to perform intergovernmental review by coordinating and reviewing federal financial assistance and direct federal development to ensure it is aligned with state and local efforts. Each state has their own requirement so find the SPOC contact for your state and call for their requirements. You will find a complete list of SPOC contacts by state in your grant or guidance. Typically they require that you send them the key information from your federal proposal, which can be submitted either by email or directly by mail.

Key Definitions - Definitions and other key terms will be important in developing your program to meet the expectations of the funder. Scan the definitions for key language or terms you may want to use in your proposal or for any terms you do not know the meaning and be sure you get clarification from the funder if needed.

Selection Criteria – The Selection Criteria section of the RFP or grant guidance explains how each section of the grant (discussed in Chapter 4) will be scored or evaluated. Most sections remain basically the same from one competition to the next, especially for government agencies. Your responses will be based on each of these sections.

Review Criteria – The standards are used to evaluate the responses you provide for each selection criteria. When developing your proposal, you should always make sure you clearly cover each of the selection and review criteria.

Checklist – The checklist includes all of the contents required for the proposal. Most times this will also provide the order in which the funder wants you to organize the proposal.

Review the Frequently Asked Questions (FAQ) section of the proposal to see if any of your questions are answered there. We suggest reading the FAQs even if you do not have any questions. Extremely valuable information can be extracted from this section. For answers to your remaining questions, search the RFP for the program contact and either call or email the contact with your questions. You might also consult with an experienced grant writer to help you fully understand the requirements of the grant.

Determine the proposal's required format

Read the guidelines for specifications about required information and how it should be arranged. You would be surprised how many great project proposals are rejected simply because the applicant did not follow instructions. Funders will often require your response be written in one of three main forms: a letter of inquiry, a proposal letter or a formal proposal submission.

A letter of inquiry should be no more than two pages, unless otherwise specified, but it should touch on all the elements that would be included in a formal proposal:

- ♣ organization/individual overview
- ♣ program information
- ♣ request for funds
- ♣ why you are a good fit with their grant-making priorities
- ♣ thank you and details about how you will follow-up
- ♣ request for permission to submit a proposal

The objective of the letter of inquiry is to get the funder to invite you to submit a full formal proposal.

Proposal letters are less formal than a lengthy proposal and contain more detail than a letter of inquiry. This type of proposal is typically two or three pages in length and often includes:

- organization/individual overview
- issue or problem that exists
- description of how you can address the problem
- request for funds
- describe the benefit to the funder

The objective of the proposal letter is to get the funder to invite you to submit a full formal proposal or to get a funder, who only contributes to pre-selected organizations/individuals, to realize you exist and possibly consider you in their future funding choices. This type of letter also may be sent to funders who have an existing connection with you or your organization.

Formal proposals or grants can vary in length and will typically include: a cover page, table of contents, abstract or executive summary, project narrative, budget narrative, budget forms, assurances and certifications and appendices or supporting documents.

Develop your proposal template

Use your RFP or grant guidelines to set up your proposal outline or template. We suggest you prepare your template and other required materials in the following steps:

Create a cover page that includes the title of the grant, the title of your program – if you have one, the deadline for submission, how the proposal is supposed to be submitted and who the program contact is. This data is all available in the RFP.

Take the application checklist or a description of application contents from the RFP and write or cut and paste the information onto the page following the cover page in the template document. This will be adjusted or cleaned-up later to be your table of contents. Be sure the Table of Contents includes the headings and subheadings of the Selection Criteria and all items contained in the Appendix.

Leave the next page blank for the abstract or executive summary. Insert any data from the RFP that outlines the abstract component requirements.

Write out or cut and paste all the Selection Criteria into the template document in the exact order in which they appear and with the exact numbered headings and subheadings – you can also include the allotted points for each.

Look at the application checklist and leave a spacer or a titled page for each additional piece of the application. Type, 'budget narrative' on a blank page, then 'budget form', then a page for each certification and assurance, then a page for each piece of the appendices.

Creating a template only takes a few minutes and will keep you organized and prevent you from leaving anything out. Even though you have spacers for the forms and appendices, etc., they will most likely not go into your template, the spacers will remind you of each form that is required. If it is a hard copy mail-in submission, you will slip the actual completed forms into the spacers later during the assembly and copying of the proposal package. If you are going to submit electronically, you will be filling out all forms and uploading any appendices online.

Set up your template in the right format as specified in the application. Small details such as 12-point font, double spacing, 1" margins, etc. are just as important as including all the information requested. Make notes in your outline regarding page limits for each section (if applicable).

The following sample may help you develop your template. Be sure to include the specific criteria questions for each of the headings so that you address each in your response.

RFP Template

Cover Page

Table of Contents

Project Abstract **(Include the project title, goals, expected outcomes and contributions for research, policy, practice, etc. Include population to be served.)**

Project Narrative **(25 single-sided, double spaced pages/12 point font or larger)**

    Statement of Need

    Project Design

    Management Plan

    Evaluation Design

Budget Narrative

    Budget Forms

Attachments/Appendix/Research

Supplementary materials, forms and research

With your template ready to go you will also need to put a plan in place for forms, appendices and research. Keep these items neat and gather them well before the deadline. Time and time again grant writers are left scrambling to pull these items together last minute – do not get stuck.

Forms

Gather any forms that are required. Required forms will either be included in the RFP or grant guidance or a link to the funder's website will be noted where you can retrieve the forms electronically. If you are using grants.gov or another electronic submission portal, the forms are filled in online. Make any notes of information you need to research, data you need to gather and any signatures required.

Attachments

Supplementary materials in your Appendix can greatly strengthen your proposal. Many funders list acceptable Appendix items. Follow their directions and do not include additional items. Include only items that enhance the proposal and are referred to in the body of the proposal, but would not, if included there, interrupt the flow of writing or put you over the allowable page limit. Do not just throw a bunch of materials in the Appendix because you can. Always make sure the items are either required or necessary to support your proposal and that each appendix or attachment is referenced in your proposal narrative. Typical Appendix items that will strengthen your proposal include: resumes or biographical sketches of key personnel, organizational charts, project partner information, additional demographic data, surveys and survey results, research or evaluation studies, and letters of support or memorandum of understanding (MOU) that directly relate to the project. Some RFPs strongly discourage attachments and make it clear that supplementary materials (e.g., videotapes, press clippings, testimonial letters) will not be reviewed. Therefore, be sure to check the guidelines for your project.

Almost all foundations require the following attachments that you can include in your Appendix:

- A copy of your IRS letter declaring tax exempt status. If your group is not tax exempt, you may need to apply through a fiscal agent, or fiscal sponsor. In that case, send a copy of your fiscal agent's IRS letter.

- A list of your board of directors and their affiliations.

- A financial statement from your last complete fiscal year, including a statement of income and expenses and a balance sheet showing assets and liabilities at the end of the year. Some funders ask for an audited statement. If you are too small to be audited, call to ask whether an audited statement is mandatory or just preferred.

- A budget for your current fiscal year.

Letters of support

If your program will be a partnership, hopefully you have already started discussions with your partner agency or better yet, you have previously collaborated on a project. Funders often favor collaborative projects. They feel it is a way to combine resources to provide the highest quality of services and ensure that the project will be sustained after the grant funding period ends. Be sure to include the partners in any major discussions, planning meetings, budget development processes and proposal reviews. Provide the partner's designated contact with materials you will need well ahead of the deadline. Guidelines often require, allow or suggest a letter of support or memorandum of understanding from your partners. These documents provide the funder with the assurance that your partner knows about the project, supports the project, and is committed to the project. Be sure to help partners draft the letter of support and discuss in advance the timing they will need to get the letter approved and signed. The Internet is a good resource to find samples of support letters and MOUs. Letters of support can also be from an 'expert' or supporter of your project detailing why he/she believes that your project should be funded.

Project design meeting

Is your head spinning yet? Imagine if you did not have our help! Well, take a break and throw a party... a design party that is. Now that you know what is required for the grant, you should identify any colleagues, participants, and administrators who will help prepare the proposal or who will provide you administrative support through the process. You may choose to have a whole grant team. Schedule a time with your team, the project partners and any other key project stakeholders to have a design meeting or conference call. Develop an agenda for the meeting:

I. Grant Overview

Review the purpose of the grant and your goals.

II. Housekeeping Items:

Develop a timeline for completing the proposal in advance of the deadline clarifying who is responsible for completion of each task and what the deadline is for each task. In addition to your own organization/individual approval and budget process, most applications will require at least one signature. This signature is authorized representative or the person who has the authority to commit contractually to the grant. Make sure that anyone who is required to sign off on the completed proposal and/or budget will be available when you are ready for final approval and signatures and incorporate their schedules into the timeline.

III. Program Development:

Begin working through your proposal template. Go through and simply answer the questions or list the items requested in each section of the selection criteria. Do not worry about full sentences, grammar, spelling, etc. at this point. Just get the ideas down.

It will help to distribute the meeting agenda prior to the meeting so that all participants come to the table prepared. This is your chance to really pick everyone's brain and lay everything out. Distribute the timeline, any notes and a list of action items from your meeting to your team.

You have planned. You are prepared. And, now…drum roll please… it is finally time to write your proposal.

Chapter 4

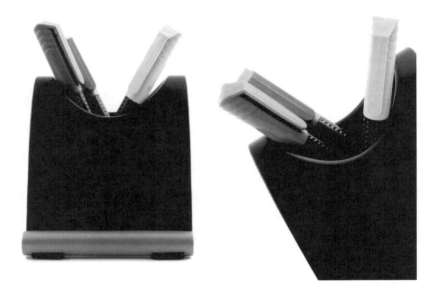

You Are Ready to Start Writing!

Really, you are ready! Take a deep breath and we will tackle each section individually so do not be overwhelmed by the whole picture.

All funders – foundation, corporate or government agency – typically request the following components:

- ♣ Cover Sheet
- ♣ Abstract or Executive Summary
- ♣ Project Narrative
- ♣ Statement of Need
- ♣ Project Design
- ♣ Management Plan
- ♣ Evaluation Design
- ♣ Budget Narrative
- ♣ Budget Forms

The order of the components, what information is requested in each section, and the page length of each of these sections will vary by funder and grant project, but the basic components are typically similar. We will address each of these sections and provide samples from successful grants to help you to visualize what a response might include.

Pre-writing Tips

A grant proposal is similar to a personal resume—you have one chance to make a good impression and grab someone's attention. Because this is the only information the reviewers have to judge your capabilities, we have compiled a list of tips to review before you get started. Consider the following tips when writing your grant:

- ♣ Follow the RFP or grant criteria exactly and place each response beneath the corresponding RFP section or subsection.

♣ Paginate the proposal narrative, and make sure that page numbers for each section and subsection correspond to those in your table of contents. Stay within the maximum number of pages required or suggested. Some funders disqualify proposals (remember my horror story in the Introduction) that exceed the limit or instruct reviewers to stop reading (and stop awarding points) once they have reached the allowable number of pages.

♣ Leave sufficient 'white space' around the narrative text by double-spacing the narrative and leaving margins on each side of at least one inch, unless the guidelines indicate otherwise.

♣ Use a font that is at least 12 point, unless the guidelines indicate otherwise.

♣ Use indentations, bold type, underlining, and bullets to make the narrative easier to read.

♣ Use charts and tables to convey information, while providing a narrative response that highlights the data's significance. Assume that the reader is not familiar with the project or with your organization/business or community.

♣ Use an acronym only after you have written out exactly what it stands for

Make the proposal interesting

♣ Tell a story (how staff will develop and deliver a particular project component; how your customers will benefit from the project).

♣ Avoid jargon like attach the thingamajig to the piffle waffle, and then add the HPQ; avoid clichés; avoid slang; and long sentences (except to avoid a choppy style).

♣ Write in easy-to-understand language. Be careful to keep the main idea themes clear – do not repeat information, keep

48

the wording simple and make appropriate use of "buzz words" that are mentioned in the criteria of the grant. If funders do not understand you, chances are they will not fund you.

* Be concrete. Do not substitute general statements or impassioned or flowery language for data and other specifics. Remember your audience; do not try to dazzle them.

* Write with an energetic and positive writing style, stating that you WILL realize the following benefits...not you HOPE to realize the following benefits... And do not beg. Remember – you are selling a winning product. Funders back winners, not losers.

Key Elements

Whew! Let's get to it! Each component of a proposal has key elements that will follow you from proposal to proposal. The instruction, tips and samples will help you integrate the information and instruction below into the template that you developed in Chapter 3.

Cover Sheet

All proposals require a cover sheet; some you will need to create and others will be a provided form. If you need to create a cover sheet, follow the funder's guidelines for what needs to be included. Typically, the following standard info is requested:

* Name of your organization/business

* Mission of your organization/business

* Organization/individual status (non-profit, educational, tribe, private corporation, small business etc.)

* Name of funder and grant program title

* Title of proposed project

* Brief one to two sentences describing the project

49

- Budget amount requesting and the specified funding period
- Name of the authorized representative
- Applicant's contact information
- Date of submission

For Federal proposals, the cover sheet is Form SF-424 or a similar form that requests specific applicant and project information. Some fields are required and some are optional; fill out the required data identified by asterisks and complete the optional data as best you can. Form SF-424 instructions will be instrumental in filling this form out. Information requested includes:

- DUNS Number and Tax Identification Number
- Contact Person: the person who is most knowledgeable about the project and proposal and is appropriate to deal with the funder regarding potentially detailed questions or budget modifications
- Catalog of Federal Domestic Assistance (CFDA) number: the identifying number of a federal program, which is sometimes preprinted on the form. You can also find the CFDA number on the first page of your RFP or proposal guidance.
- Descriptive Title of the Applicant's Project
- Geographic areas affected by the project
- Congressional district(s) of the applicant and of the project/program
- Estimated Funding
- Contact information and signature of the Applicant's Authorized Representative

Abstract or Executive Summary

This one-page summary provides an overview of the entire proposal and precedes the proposal narrative. Check for specific information the funder requests to be included in the abstract. Although it is the last thing you write, it is probably the first thing read, so make it clear, specific, and interesting.

Each RFP or grant contains a slightly different description of the required summary or abstract. In general, the abstract should briefly describe:

- the location of the project
- the needs being addressed
- the number and type of participants to be served
- project goals and objectives
- activities/approaches
- intended project outcomes

Sample Abstract

The Happy Kids Public School District (HPSD) project, **East Meets West: Traditional American History for Happy Town Teachers** is a three-year professional development program designed to improve teacher knowledge of traditional American history content, including presentations by professional historians, reading and analyzing of primary and secondary sources, and development of specific lesson plans and history classes based on learning that arises from the sessions. Academic and public historians will lead teachers through sessions and courses, and learning specialists and master teachers will work with HPSD teachers to help them deliver traditional themes and topics of American history to students in their classrooms.

East Meets West will immerse 24 elementary and middle school teachers and 11 high school American history teachers in content learning and content-based teaching strategies through training in historical thinking grounded in the following elements: 1) using primary and secondary resources; 2) formulating questions through inquiry and determining their importance; 3) analyzing how historians use evidence and artifacts; 4) understanding how historians develop differing interpretations; 5) examining bias and points of view; 6) understanding historical debate and controversy; 7) examining how causation relates to continuity and change; 8) discovering the interrelationships among themes, regions and time periods; and 9) learning that any understanding of the past requires an understanding of the assumptions and the values of the past.

The project includes formal partnerships with leaders in the field of American History Education:

- ¬ Intensive history content teacher training provided by the Smith Council for History Education and Jones Company

- ¬ American History seminars taught by the University of Happy Town

- ¬ District vertical team sharing across clusters

- ¬ Collaboration with three local museums: The RST Cultural Center, The UVW Museum of Art and History and The National XYZ Museum

The program outcomes include higher levels of student engagement in extant American history courses, as well as evidence of teachers employing new methods of engaging students and imparting facts in cluster school classes. Student achievement will improve, which will be evaluated and measured through testing.

Need Statement

The Need Statement describes the needs to be addressed by the project. This includes the impact of the needs on the target audience as well as on the community/service area as a whole. This section is an important part of the proposal because funders must be convinced and agree that a critical condition or significant need exists. Funders are motivated to help when a compelling need exists.

A formal or informal needs assessment will be instrumental in writing your proposal's Need Statement. An assessment may include research (questionnaires, surveys, and focus groups), observation, anecdotes, review of literature in the field, and demographic and/or statistical data. The information provided should be both factual and directly related to the problem addressed by the proposal. Areas to document are:

- The purpose for developing the proposal.

- The beneficiaries -- who are they and how will they benefit.

- The social and economic costs to be affected.

- The nature of the problem (provide as much hard evidence as possible).

- How the applicant came to realize the problem exists, and what is currently being done about the problem.

- The specific manner through which problems might be solved.

Review the resources needed, considering how they will be used and to what end. The need statement should be well supported with evidence and examples. Always assume the reader may not be familiar with the community, your organization or the project. Use these tips when writing your needs statement:

♣ State the need using hard-core statistics; never make assumptions

♣ Use selective, relevant, and comparative statistics that demonstrate the magnitude of the problem

♣ Quote authorities who have spoken on your topic

♣ Use anecdotes as examples

♣ Use, where appropriate, observations about needs with references to recent research

♣ Focus on the need of the geographic area you can serve

♣ Give a clear sense of the urgency of your request

♣ Link needs within the context of the funder agency's own statements of need.

♣ Do not overwhelm the reader with statistics, use clear tables or charts that contain carefully selected data, as well as a narrative that underscores critical points about the data's significance.

Sample Needs Statement

Students who know and appreciate the great ideas, issues and events of American History are more likely to understand and exercise their civic rights and responsibilities.[1] With this concept in mind, districts serving a high number of first and second generation Americans have a duty to ensure effective teaching of American history. Happy Kids School District (HKSD) District is such a district – and this funding would help us to meet this obligation.

With 448,607 residents (more than 30% of the state's population),[2] Happy is the largest city in Happy Town. Serving approximately 91,000 students across 148 schools, HKSD is the largest public school district in Happy Town, and the 31st largest in the United States.[3] Although classified as a Metro (inner city) district, total federal revenues for the district are lower than state and national averages. In fact, in 2005, HKSD' total revenue from federal dollars equaled only $663 per student, as compared to $1,246 per student statewide and $773 nationwide.[4] Because of its location in the Southwest, HKSD serves a higher percentage (4.8%) of Native American students than many larger school districts in the country, where the norm is usually less than 1%. Additionally, HKSD serves a large Latino population (52%), many of whom speak Spanish as their first and home language.

---

[1] Department of Education, Teaching American History Grant, 2003.
[2] *Census 2000*
[3] U.S. Department of Education, 2001
[4] NCES, 2005

The geographic setting of the district in the Southwest suggests a removal from much of the American history that occurred in the East and Midwest. Yet the demographic make-up of the district's student population lends itself to cultivating high interest in many of the key threads of traditional American history, such as conflicts between indigenous peoples and colonialism, immigration, and the birth and evolution of a nation seeking to provide freedom and justice for diverse populations.

Our proposed project, **East Meets West: Traditional American History for Happy Town Teachers**, is a three-year professional development program designed to improve teacher knowledge of traditional American history content, including presentations by professional historians, reading and analyzing of primary and secondary sources, and development of specific lesson plans and history classes based on learning that arises from the sessions. Academic and public historians will lead teachers through sessions and courses, and learning specialists and master teachers will work with teachers to help them deliver traditional themes and topics of American history to students in their classrooms.

Because HKSD is such a large district and divided into 11 clusters, there is a problem in the district as a whole with consistency. The teachers of American History trained through *East Meets West*, acting as emissaries, will take a consistent body of history content into the schools.

East Meets West will immerse 24 elementary and middle school teachers and 11 high school American history teachers in content learning and content-based teaching strategies through training in historical thinking grounded in the following elements: 1) using primary and secondary resources; 2) formulating questions through inquiry and determining their importance; 3) analyzing how historians use evidence and artifacts; 4) understanding how historians develop differing interpretations; 5) examining bias and points of view; 6) understanding historical debate and controversy; 7) examining how causation relates to continuity and change; 8) discovering the interrelationships among themes, regions and time periods; and 9) learning that any understanding of the past requires an understanding of the assumptions and the values of the past.

In addition to these professional development benchmarks, a second goal of *East Meets West* is to train teachers how to engage their students and guide them past geographic and local barriers so that they move beyond Happy and "see" the nation and the relevance of American history in an ever-changing modern world.

The project will address the most challenging issue faced by HKSD in its efforts to educate students in American history: **most secondary history teachers in HKSD classrooms have a social studies certification but do not necessarily have a major or minor in American history**. Consequently, most HKSD teachers lack specific knowledge of traditional American history. *East Meets West* seeks to provide teachers a basic understanding of the American past.

Invitational Priority One

East Meets West is specifically designed to provide professional development for elementary through eighth grade teachers in schools that have not made Adequate Yearly Progress (AYP). Out of 83 elementary schools at HKSD, 37 have not made AYP; 21 out of 27 middle schools and 9 out of 11 high schools in the district are also deficient, scoring less than proficient on the Happy Town Standards-Based Assessment set by the HT Public Education Department.

East Meets West has been designed by a diverse planning team of teachers, administrators and community partners to develop a sustainable and rigorous district-wide American history academic program that will meet (and *exceed)* the Happy Town American history standards. The program activities focus on content and content-related teaching strategies in American history.

Project Design

The Project Design section – your plan of action – is often reviewed the closest, not to mention assigned the most points in the review process. The Project Design demonstrates in detail how you will meet the need identified in your Needs Statement.

Goals and Objectives

GOALS are broad-based statements about the changes your project will bring about. Goals may be your funding goals from Chapter 1– where you want to go, or you may have modified them during the planning process. Link goals to the funder agency's project purposes and incorporate into your goals' key "buzz" words used by the funder. Your project might have a primary or overall goal and some sub-goals. Include at least one goal for each key project component or activity.

OBJECTIVES are measurable, time-specific results/outcomes that your project will attain. Your stated objectives will be used to evaluate program progress, so be realistic. Answer the following questions when writing your objectives: Who is affected (target audience)? How much is the target audience affected in measurable terms? During what time period this effect or change will occur?

When writing your objectives consider the following:

* ♣ Each objective should relate directly to your goals.

* ♣ Indicate by when participants will have achieved each objective.

* ♣ State objectives in terms of outcomes, in terms of activities or methods.

* ♣ State objectives in quantifiable terms. Use such words as reduce, increase, decrease, and gain; indicate by how much or by what percentage.

* ♣ Determine how you will measure the change you describe under each objective.

* ♣ Identify the population for each objective.

- ♣ Develop objectives for each major activity.

- ♣ Select a realistic time frame for each objective that allows ample time to accomplish it.

- ♣ Funders sometimes require or suggest that you demonstrate that project participants show greater improvement than a comparable group of non-participants - cohorts.

Multi-year projects require multi-year objectives. Decide how much change you can expect in each year. Indicate a clear timeframe so that the reader can see whether you expect the objective to be attained at the end, for example, of Year One or Year Three (or at the end of each project year).

Number your objectives, so you can more clearly refer to them in your evaluation section. As a result of the Government Performance and Results Act (GPRA) of 1993, each federal agency must list objectives and measurable performance indicators for each program. Use each program's performance indicators as a basis for developing your own objectives.

Sample Goals and Objectives

East Meets West will offer teachers more than a three-year immersion in the study of American history content. Teachers will also develop skills in historical research and learn the importance of collegial partnership with their fellow teachers as they learn and practice effective teaching strategies to incorporate in their classrooms. The project will create a critical systemic change with the following hoped for results: 1) improve teacher instructional strategies that support and facilitate standards-based instruction in traditional American history; 2) make American history relevant to students in the Southwest, whose cultural background differs from youth on the East coast and for whom the original colonies and early American history may feel unfamiliar and remote; 3) connect locales in Happy Town and the Southwest to the larger picture of historic events unfolding in the nation as a whole; 4) improve teacher understanding of the importance of place in American history; and 5) establish vertical American history teaching teams that will foster professional development and teacher collaboration and collegiality and that will sustain and enhance teacher learning in the subject in the post grant years.

East Meets West will seek to achieve the following results, or measurable outcomes:

1) Students at the 5th, 8th, and 11th grade levels will show evidence of comprehension of American history course content as measured by pre- and post-tests;

2) Student American history studies at the 5th, 8th, and 11th grade levels will culminate in the completion of a student product to be determined by the vertical teams (in collaboration with other teachers) for each cluster; and

3) Increase in the number of students completing Advanced Placement American History and increase in the number of students successfully taking the AP test.

Activities

The activities proposed in your project/program are the tools for accomplishing goals and objectives. They indicate how goals and objectives will be attained. Be sure to lay out all the details for the funder. Use the following guidelines in selecting activities and describing them in the project design:

Select activities that are identified by the funder as required or as priorities.

Select activities that will clearly have a positive impact on participants and are directly related to your program goals and objectives. Each activity should correlate to one or more objectives and to a previously identified need.

Select activities that involve the different members of the target audience/area.

Select activities that are reasonable in terms of the budget, project time frame, number of participants, staff and other resources.

Include activities that are designed to build capacity.

Describing Activities

Describe the content of each activity. Make each activity's appropriateness clear and indicate the research and other rationales for selecting methodology. F or educational organizations, relate each activity, where feasible, to State Content Learning Standards, Performance Standards, strategic plan, and any priorities contained in the RFP. For each activity, clearly indicate:

- ♣ Exactly who will participate.

- ♣ How you will choose the target group.

- ♣ The number of participants in each activity to make clear whether staffing and other resources are sufficient to serve them and communicates the overall scope of the project.

- ♣ The title of the person(s) responsible for carrying out each activity. Use active, rather than passive, constructions. For example, 'The Project Director (grant-funded) will conduct (active voice) ….

- ♣ The schedule of each activity: time, length, duration, frequency.

- ♣ The location of each activity, so that the funder can see the use the project will make of facilities.

Program activities can be described in a narrative form, and can also be described in a chart that specifies, for each activity, its timeframe, description, participants, and titles of the responsible person(s).

Research

Some RFPs and grants contain a separate section that asks you to describe the research basis of your project. Most often, RFPs contain no explicit reference to research, but do expect you to respond, with reference to research and best practices, to questions about the program design, appropriateness of services, and the likelihood that your program will address the need/problem and meet the project/program goals. Is the program or activity you are proposing to meet your identified need a research-based or scientifically proven model? Is there research demonstrating effectiveness of your concept? Have you conducted any studies and what were the results? A funder might also request that you include a summary in the appendix of any evaluation studies, reports or research that may document the effectiveness of success of the activities/services proposed.

When documenting research in your proposal, keep the focus on your description of your approach and strategies by placing the citation itself in parenthesis or using footnotes. If allowed, put together a bibliography or a list of citations to include in your appendix.

Project Management Plan

The management plan describes to the funder how your organization/business is structured and how the program will be managed. This section of the proposal should convince the funder that you are dedicated and committed to the project and you have capacity to manage all the program and financial aspects of the project. Consider the following steps when writing your management plan:

- ♣ Determine who will have day-today administrative and supervisory responsibility for the project.

- ♣ List the primary responsibilities of key project staff as it relates to your project activities.

- ♣ Include the range of essential administrative, supervisory, and coordinating responsibilities, such as staff supervision, liaison to funders and the evaluator, meeting reporting requirements, fiscal management, and articulating with partners as well as community groups.

- ♣ Describe experience and qualifications of management and key project personnel.

Think through the steps needed for proper management of the project. These steps might include: regularly scheduled meetings between and among the project director, coordinators, project staff, and consultants (including the evaluator), and meetings of the leadership, management or advisory team. Specify the frequency of each type of meeting. If there is no space restriction or limit on what may be included in the Appendix, include an organizational or staffing chart for the project, as well as resumes of key staff and refer to these attachments in the project management section.

Timeline

Your timeline should provide the funder with a step-by-step plan to accomplish each activity/component you have proposed – what you intend to do and when. The timeline should be a clear and logical sequence of activities and can be presented in several different formats. Multi-year projects require multi-year timelines. Use the following guidelines when designing your project timeline:

- ♣ Include the major activities discussed in the narrative.

- ♣ Provide a completion or execution date and who will be responsible for each activity.

- ♣ Identify any ongoing activities (e.g. evaluation) in the beginning.

- ♣ Highlight or identify project milestones.

- ♣ Include who will complete the task and any participants.

Sample Management Plan

Adequacy of the management plan and timeline. The project management plan is designed to ensure sustainability and success. HKSD has successfully implemented federally funded projects in the past, achieving objectives on time and within budget. Upon award notification, the following timeline will serve as a benchmark measurement for program progress (the *East Meets West* Steering Committee will finalize timeline details when awarded).

Timeframe Years 1-3	Tasks and Milestones	Responsibility
August	Year 1: Awards Announced; Project director appointed. Select project secretary; Steering Committee Meeting 1: Launch discussion; review of program goals/objectives. Implementation plan established. Materials and supplies ordered. Year 2: 2-day vertical team debriefing/implementation meeting. Year 3: 2-day vertical team debriefing/project presentation and future implementation meeting; Press release.	Steering Committee, HKSD District Administration
September	35 teacher participants selected. Vertical team leaders appointed. Contractor agreements finalized; all PD activities scheduled.	Project Director
October	Vertical team meetings begin. Facilitator training provided to vertical team leaders in Year 1; Years 2-3 regular vertical team meetings. Final UHT seminar roster created; distributed to teachers. Sign-up/enrollment begins.	Project Director Carol Black Pat Brown (year 1)

November	Steering committee meeting #2; Substitutes arranged (half day Friday subs and full-day Saturday) provided for teachers to attend UHT seminars. **Milestone: UHT seminars begin.**	Project Director; UHT
January	UHT seminars (2); preparation for agenda/materials for museum vertical team meeting.	Project Director; UHT; Proj Asst
February	Local museum vertical team meeting	Museum; Project Director
March	Announcement of Jones Company two-day workshop.	Project Asst
April	**Milestone: Jones Company two-day workshop.**	Jones Company facilitator
May/June	**Milestone: SCHE five-day Colloquium**	SCHE
July	**Milestone: Jones Company Summer Institute.**	Jones Company
August	2-day vertical team implementation meetings. Debrief summer activities and plan implementation strategies.	Project Director; Project Asst

Adequacy of time commitment for director and staff. As project director, Sue Jones will commit 100% of her time to this project. She will contract, coordinate and oversee all professional development training; work with teachers, administrators, and counselors to implement the program components; report on progress to the school

64

board; and manage the budget. She will work with committee members to share program progress and make adjustments to the program as needed to ensure program success. Martha will also coordinate the consultant activities. (See above for a full description of the structure of the project, project roles, and the expectations for the consultants.)

Additional management support will be provided by a part-time secretary. The secretary will be hired to provide clerical support for the project director and key staff. Carol Black will be contracted to serve as the library consultant/program assistant for the project and will contribute approximately 2 days per week (420 hours total) each year of the project to provide primary source training and maintain a library of resources and program materials.

The *East Meets West* Steering Committee will be comprised of teacher representatives, Dr. Scharff from UHT, Kim Whites, Sue Jones, and Carol Black. They will meet three times in each project year. SCHE representatives will be invited to attend a special evaluation at the end of the first year. During the life of the grant, release time and collaborative time will be provided to the teacher participants so that cluster vertical teams, in conjunction with the grade level leaders, will have ample opportunity to meet, plan and share. Substitute teachers have been budgeted to cover teacher classrooms during these times.

Evaluation

Evaluation is an important and integral part of a proposal. The evaluation plan describes how you will assess the impact, successes and/or failures of the project and the project's effectiveness in meeting the project goals and objectives. The evaluation component is two-fold: (1) product evaluation; and (2) process evaluation. Product evaluation addresses results that can be attributed to the project, as well as the extent to which the project has satisfied its desired objectives. Process evaluation addresses how the project was conducted, in terms of consistency with the stated plan of action and the effectiveness of the various activities within the plan. Funders are increasingly interested in supporting only projects that are demonstrating effectiveness and making clear progress toward meeting their goals. Evaluation activities begin at the start of the program and are ongoing throughout the program. They end with the final evaluation report, which is usually submitted within 90 days after the program's completion (summative).

An effective evaluation section will identify the evaluator and briefly provide the evaluator's qualifications; indicate the extent to which the project will meet its objectives; describe evaluation instruments, data collection methods and data analysis processes; demonstrate how the evaluation will contribute to improving the program; and describe the evaluation reports to be produced.

Describe your plan to report these results: how, when, and to whom. Describe how project staff will use the findings to modify and improve the program in an ongoing way (formative evaluation), not just at the end of each project year.

One way to communicate information about evaluation activities is through a chart that clearly shows each objective, the evaluation instrument used to determine whether that objective has been met, and the timeframe for collecting each type of data.

Evaluation Design Sample

The evaluation will be a collaborative venture between the evaluator and project personnel. The evaluation design will be presented at the initial *East Meets West* Steering Committee meeting and revised to incorporate suggestions and feedback from project personnel, such as the project director and the vertical team grade level leaders. This collaboration will result in the best possible evaluation design and the buy-in necessary to implement the evaluation. The goals of the evaluation are: 1) to provide valid information that documents the implementation of the project and explains outcomes (qualitative evaluation), and 2) to evaluate the impact of the project on teachers and students and determine if project goals and objectives have been achieved (quantitative evaluation). The evaluation design utilizes objective performance measures, both qualitative and quantitative, which are described in more detail below. The formative (or qualitative) evaluation, which includes benchmarks to monitor progress toward specific project activities, is presented first, followed by the summative (or quantitative) evaluation which includes outcome measures to assess the impact of the project on teachers and students. A table at the end of the evaluation section summarizes how each of the pieces of the evaluation fits together and meets the criterion for the quality of the project evaluation.

Formative Evaluation. The formative evaluation, which is primarily qualitative in nature, will describe the implementation of the project and will provide the project director and steering committee with regular feedback via e-mail, phone conversations, meetings, and reports about the effectiveness of project activities. This feedback will enable revision and improvement of the professional development model as it is implemented. The qualitative evaluation includes three primary ways to provide benchmarks to monitor progress towards project implementation.

Participant-Observation. The evaluator will be a participant observer at primary grant activities such as summer institutes, seminars, and vertical team meetings, and will provide information about these through observation and compilation of results of evaluation surveys administered at each professional development activity.

Content Review. The evaluator also will review all written information documenting the implementation of the project such as vertical team meeting minutes, correspondence, print materials, and other written or web-based publications.

Implementation Journaling. In a meta-analysis of effective teaching, Stronge (2002) indicates that teacher reflection is a vital part of effective teaching. Reflection is a careful review of one's own teaching, involving critical thinking that can lead to increased teacher efficacy, thereby influencing students' attitudes and achievement. Reflective thinking about the teaching of American history will be facilitated through vertical team meetings and the use of journals in which teachers will record their thoughts and ideas on how and where they could implement information they learn. "Implementation journals" will document participation in professional development activities (colloquia, seminars, vertical team meetings); changes in instructional techniques and student assessment strategies; and the impact of these changes on students.

The journal also will include products produced by teacher participants, such as American history units, lesson plans, alternative assessment instruments, etc.

Summative Evaluation. Comprehensive teacher knowledge of the subject matter and how to convey this subject matter to students is a core component of teacher preparation standards from professional organizations. Therefore, the quantitative evaluation will focus on: 1) teacher knowledge of American history, 2) changes in instructional strategies and assessment practices, and 3) the impact of the project on student engagement and achievement in American history.

Teacher Content Knowledge. Teacher knowledge of American history will be evaluated by examining the accuracy and sophistication of connections between American and Southwestern history as reflected in the Implementation Journals and instructional units prepared by teachers. In addition, the evaluator will work closely with SCHE, UHT, and Jones Company to collect information about teacher subject matter knowledge through anecdotal evidence provided by professional development providers/facilitators as well as through any evaluation data they may routinely collect. Pre- and post- teacher surveys will also be designed and implemented.

Teaching and Assessment Practices. Changes in instructional strategies and assessment practices of teachers participating in the grant will be measured with a pre/post-survey, content review of teacher Implementation Journals, and analysis of instructional units developed by teachers. The survey, which will be administered to teachers retrospectively at the end of each year of participation in the grant, will ask teachers to report how much time they spent using a wide variety of teaching and assessment strategies, both prior to, and after participation in the grant. The survey will be developed by the evaluator in collaboration with project personnel and will be based on research regarding best practices in teaching and assessment, recommendations of national history organizations, and the specific goals of the grant. In addition to the teacher survey, instructional units prepared by teachers will be scored by master teachers who have been trained in the use of rubrics. Scoring will focus on the accuracy and breadth of historical content, the use of a variety of resources, strategies for active student engagement, and alternative assessment strategies. A sample of Implementation Journals will be reviewed by the evaluator for more in-depth evidence and understanding of changes in teacher instructional and assessment practices. Group evaluation sessions with vertical team representatives and leaders may be used.

Student Achievement. The impact of the grant on students will be measured through student products, teacher assessment, history examination results for students in grades 5, 8, and 11, and changes in AP U.S. History enrollments and pass rates on exams. On surveys, teachers will be asked to report changes they have noticed in their classrooms as a result of altering their teaching of history, for example, changes in student motivation, engagement, attendance, etc. They also will provide information on student achievement, which may include anecdotal evidence as well as the results of classroom assessments, such as performances, tests, projects, grades, etc. Although standardized tests are often considered to be the most important indicator of a teacher's impact on students, in reality, teacher-created assignments and assessments are probably the most relevant (Guskey, 2003). It is necessary to first document that teachers have changed their teaching practices before measurement of student impact through testing.

Benchmarks and Outcomes Table

Benchmarks & Outcomes 4a, 4b, 4c	Instruments 4e (iv)	Type of Data 4e (i)	Collection Methods & Dates 4e(ii) &(iii)	Analysis 4e(v) Qual/Quan	Outcomes Available 4e(vi)
Teacher content knowledge	Implementa-tion journal	Qualitative	Vertical Team Meetings	X	Quarterly
	Prof Dev Evaluations	Scales, Open-ended	End of each Prof Dev activity	X X	1 month after
	Instructional units	Scoring Rubric	End of each year	X X	Annual report
Teaching & Assessment Practices	Teacher Survey	Pre-Post Self-ratings	End of each year	X X	Annual Report
	Instructional Units	Scoring Rubric	End of each year	X X	Annual Report
	Implementation Journal	Content Analysis	End of each year	X	Annual Report

Benchmarks & Outcomes 4a, 4b, 4c	Instruments 4e (iv)	Type of Data 4e (i)	Collection Methods & Dates 4e(ii) &(iii)	Analysis 4e(v) Qual/Quan		Outcomes Available 4e(vi)
	Vertical Team Interviews	Qualitative	Vertical Team Meeting	X		Annual Report
Student Achievement	Student Products	Rubric	End of each year		X	Annual Report
	Teacher Survey	Grades, Observa-tions	End of each year	X	X	Annual Report
	Student History Exams	Pre/Post Scores	Final year of grant		X	Annual Report
	AP History Enrollment/ Exams	Percentages, Pass Rates	End of each year		X	Annual Report

Evaluator

Government funders may expect you to use an outside evaluator who has not been involved in planning the project and will not be involved in its operation. Talk to colleagues about their experiences with various evaluators, while remembering that a good evaluation is not necessarily a glowing program assessment. Choose an evaluator who has adequate time to give to your project and who has relevant expertise and experience. If you provide detailed information about the proposed project activities, the evaluator might help you develop your proposal's evaluation section, as well as provide feedback on your measurable objectives.

Budget

Proposal budgets typically consist of both a budget narrative and a completed budget form that just includes the categorical totals for the project. Carefully read the directions regarding budget, paying attention to any instructions about mandatory costs and/or unallowable costs. Be realistic. Under-budgeting will impact the overall success of you carrying out your project. Over-estimating your budget can appear to the funder that you may have not done your due diligence in setting realistic costs.

Begin the budgeting process by reviewing each project component and make a list of possible costs, including personnel, fringe benefits, travel, supplies, equipment, contractor costs and stipends. A multi-year budget and budget narrative must accompany a multi-year project request.

<u>Sample Budget Narrative</u>

1. <u>Personnel</u>

Sue Jones will serve as the full-time project director. Her annual salary for each year of the grant project will be $65,000.

A half-time secretary will be hired at an annual rate of $11,750, based on the annual salary of $23,500. This annual rate is based on HKSD' district salary schedule level for the position.

Total personnel Years 1-3: $76,750

2. <u>Fringe Benefits</u>

The fringe benefit cost to the project was based on total salaries and wages for the project director for years 1-3 based on the district's cumulative rate of .290. (No fringe benefits for the part-time secretary.) This rate is broken down as follows:

ERA   .0940

ERA- retirement health   .020

FICA   .0660

Medicare/FICA   .0145

Health/medical   .09

Workers Comp   .005

Total Fringe Benefits Years 1-3: $ 65,000 X .290 = $18,850

3. Travel:

Project Director and 1 other staff member (TBD) will travel to the mandatory two-day annual meeting of the Teaching American History Grant program in Washington D.C. each year of the project. Costs were estimated based on Internet travel prices for round-trip airfare and lodging and the district's per-diem rate.

> Airfare: $650 X 2 staff = $1,300
>
> Per Diem: $100 X 3 days X 2 staff = $ 600
>
> Lodging: $150 X 3 days X 2 staff = $ 900

Jones Company Teacher Institute – 12 elementary and middle school teachers will travel to Jones Company during the grant years to participate in a two-day the Teacher Institute in Early American History. Each teacher will be paid a stipend of $500 toward travel expenses. 12 teachers X $500 = $6,000

> Total travel costs Years 1-3: $8,800

4.   Equipment – $0

5. <u>Supplies:</u> Adequate materials and supplies will be required for each grant participant as detailed below. Additional copies of materials are being budgeted to provide the teachers and key staff with resource copies, as well as to allow for new history teachers that may come to the district during the three year grant. The portfolios will be purchased each year so that teachers can build a resource of materials and information they receive each year of the grant. The costs are based on actual vendor and/or contractor quotes:

Thinking Historically - 40 copies x $15.95/copy = $638 (Year 1 only) (recalculate)

Social Studies Vertical Team Guides - 40 copies x $35/copy = $1,400 (Year 1 only)

Materials for UHT seminars @ 40 copies x $200 = $8,000

Portfolio for teacher implementation journaling - $19 X 38 = $722

Total cost of supplies Year 1: $10,760

Total cost of supplies Year 2-3: $8,722

6. <u>Contractual:</u>

SCHE's five-day colloquium (5-day program, 3-person leadership team) will cost $45,270, based on a total customized program estimate provided by the contractor (see attached MOU for detail).

(3) UHT 10-hour seminars each year of the project (quote provided by UHT) is budgeted at $1,000 per seminar. This cost includes the professor time for instruction. 3 seminars x $2,500 each = $7,500.

Jones Company 2-day professional development workshops will be presented each year of the grant. The cost for the workshops per year (quote provided by Jones Company) = $16,775

12 middle and elementary teachers from the teacher cohort will travel to City, State each year of the grant to participate in the **Jones Company Summer Institute**. The cost per teacher is $1,800. (An additional $500 per teacher has been budgeted in the travel line item to support this activity). 12 teachers X $1,800 = $21,600.

Dr. Jill Smith, UHT, will be paid a **stipend** of $1,000 per year for her contribution to the steering committee.

The cost of **Kim White, evaluation services**, is calculated based the estimate for services outlined in Section 4 of the narrative and represents approximately 10% of the total overall budget, which is reasonable considering the value of services provided. The evaluation cost for each year of the grant is $30,000.

Carol Black will be contracted to serve as the library consultant/program assistant for each year of the grant (see duties described in grant narrative). She will work approximately 420 hours per year at a rate of $25 per hour for a total cost of $10,500 per year.

Pat Brown will provide facilitation training to team leaders during Year 1 only of the project at a total cost of $3,500 (including $1,800 for consultation services; $1,200 for travel expenses and $500 for training materials).

Total contractual Year 1: $136,145

Total contractual Years 2-3: $132,645

7. Construction – there are no construction costs associated with this project.

8. Other

Substitute teacher pay for 3.5 days per year will be required so that participant teachers can attend the following meetings. Cost is based on the district daily substitute rate of $80/$40 for a half-day. *Every effort has been made to schedule Saturday and summer activities to minimize the amount of time that teachers are out of their classrooms and also to keep the cost of substitute pay at a minimum.*

1st Vertical Team meeting (Pat Brown) – 38 teachers X $85 = $3,230

UHT Seminars (1/2-day; Friday afternoon) – 38 teachers X $40 = $1,520

Local museum vertical team meeting – 38 teachers X $80 = $3,040

Jones Company Workshop (Friday) –38 teachers X $80 = $3,040

Total Other costs Years 1-3: $10,830

9. Direct Costs: The total direct costs (budget categories 1-8 above):

Total Direct Costs Year 1: $262,135

Total Direct Costs Years 2-3: $245,767

10. Indirect costs

The district's indirect cost rate is .0205.

> Total Indirect Costs Year 1: $5,374
>
> Total Indirect Costs Years 2-3: $5,038

11. Training Stipends:

Teacher training stipends have been estimated based on the district's stipend rate of $18 X 110 hours = $1,980 X 38 teachers = $75,240. This amount includes attendance at all activities beyond the school day (52 hours) with the remaining time (58 hours) for teacher preparation for school meetings, lesson development, and meetings with the library consultant/project assistant and Project Director.

Vertical team representatives (3) will receive an additional $2,000 per year beyond their participation stipend above - for their planning, consulting and facilitation time for a total of $6,000 per year.

> Total training stipends Years 1-3: $81,240

12. Total Costs

> Total costs Year 1: $348,749
>
> Total costs Years 2-3: $332,045

Section A: Budget Summary

Budget Categories	Project Year One	Project Year Two	Project Year Three
1. Personnel	$76,750	$76,750	$76,750
2. Fringe Benefits	$18,850	$18,850	$18,850
3. Travel	$8,800	$8,800	$8,800
4. Equipment	0	0	0
5. Supplies	$10,760	$8,722	$8,722
6. Contractual	$136,145	$132,645	$132,645
7. Construction	0	0	0
8. Other	$10,830	$10,830	$10,830
9. Total Direct Costs (lines 1-8)	$262,135	$245,767	$245,767
10. Indirect Costs	$5,374	$5,038	$5,038
11. Training Stipends	$81,240	$81,240	$81,240
12. Total Costs (lines 9 - 11)	$348,749	$332,045	$332,045

Review

Once all of the components are complete, take the time to thoroughly review each section, including all required forms and attachments. Ask someone unfamiliar with the proposal to proofread for typographical and other errors. You can also hire a professional grant writer to review your proposal for both grammar, flow and more importantly, that your proposal fully addresses all the criteria areas of the narrative response. A professional grant writer can also give you suggestions on how to strengthen sections of your grant proposal and might catch other requirements that are often missed, such as including mandatory travel to grantee meetings in your budget, or clearly identifying priority areas that the funder has identified. Our team has adopted a strict 'no-ego' policy – we all think we're brilliant writers at 4a.m., but a second set of eyes will almost always find small errors that we missed.

Chapter 5

Submitting your Proposal

Pat yourself on the back...You have prepared a work of art, you made it! So how the heck do you get rid of it? Your grant RFP or guidelines will specify the method of submission and instructions on how the proposal should be packaged and when it is due. Use the checklist provided in the RFP, you may need to create one, to make sure your application is complete before it is submitted. Here is an example pulled from a U.S. Department of Education program RFP:

Application Transmittal Instructions

Applications for grants under this grant competition may be submitted electronically or in paper format by mail or hand delivery. The electronic submission of applications is voluntary. However, if you choose to submit your application electronically you must use the site listed below. Note: You may not submit your application by e-mail or facsimile.

Applications Submitted Electronically

You must submit your grant application through the Internet using the software provided on the Grants.gov Web site (www.grants.gov) by 4:30 p.m. (Washington, DC time) on the application deadline date.

Application Preparation Checklist

Application for Federal Assistance (SF Form 424) is completed according to the instructions and includes the nine-digit D-U-N-S Number and Tax Identification Number.

All required forms are signed in black or blue ink and dated by an authorized official and the signed original is included with your submission.

One signed original and two copies of the application, including all required forms and appendices plus one voluntarily submitted additional copy, are included. All copies are unbound and each page is consecutively numbered.

Deadline Date: **May 21, 2007**. See Sections I and IV of this application package for complete application transmittal instructions and general application instructions and information.

- θ Application for Federal Assistance (SF Form 424)
- θ Department of Education Supplemental Information Form for the SF 424
- θ Project Abstract (one page maximum)
- θ Project Narrative (up to 25 pages double-spaced)
- θ Program-Specific Assurance
- θ Competitive Preference Qualification Assurance, if applicable
- θ Partner Agreements
- θ All applications must include the required forms, assurances, and certifications, including:
  - θ Budget Information Form (ED Form 524) and detailed budget narrative
  - θ Assurances, Non-Construction Programs (ED Form 424B)
  - θ Disclosure of Lobbying Activities (Standard Form– LLL)

    NOTE: The Authorized Representative must sign this form even if it is not applicable to the applicant
  - θ Grants.gov Lobbying Form

- θ Narrative response to GEPA 427

- θ Copy of letter to State Single Point of Contact

- θ Proof of federally negotiated indirect cost rate (if claiming indirect costs)

If you want to apply for a grant and be considered for funding, you must meet the deadline requirements and follow the funder's directions. Allow plenty of time for production and submission. Consider enlisting a member of your grant team, if applicable, or office support staff to assist you. Being up against a time crunch through the final stages of packaging and/or submitting your application increases the chances for mistakes and can prevent you from being able to deal with unexpected last-minute complications or technical difficulties/glitches can often arise. Believe us, we know first hand!

One of the writers on my team shares her grant submittal horror story:

"Back before federal agencies changed from the courier truck to electronic transmittal, I submitted a 300 page (narrative and attachments) Magnet Schools Assistance Program proposal for three different clients and the submission instructions included: one full original copy not bound, signatures in blue only, two full copies bound with binder clips, two optional extra copies of just the project narrative bound with binder clips only, no binders or staples... *up hill both ways in the snow, barefoot.* The photocopier would jam or run out of paper and paper was everywhere. The last courier pick-up was at 3p.m. and I was filling out three mailing labels at 3pm and had to drive an hour to the only station in the city that had a 6 p.m. pick-up. It was a catastrophe! Once the package was safely on its way... RELIEF."

This last minute craziness can happen to anyone. Do not underestimate the process; plan properly to do it right!

Methods of submission

There are three methods to submit your grant: 1) paper format by mail or courier; 2) paper format via hand delivery; and 3) electronic submission. For most government grants, both paper format methods are being phased out and replaced with electronic submission systems. Most states have their own electronic systems and most federal grants will be submitted through Grants.gov. Grants.gov is the main source to find and apply for federal government grants. Foundations and corporations tend to accept mailed hard copy paper applications and can occasionally have online applications.

Paper submission

When submitting your proposal in hard copy form, we suggest preparing a cover or transmittal letter. This should outline a very brief overview of the project, who the partners are (if any) and why the funding for this proposal is crucial to your program. DO convey liveliness and enthusiasm in your letter and presentation. Remember - you are selling! Make the funder want to buy.

Make an extra hard copy of the entire final package and any submission documents for your files. You will regularly refer to the final proposal to answer any questions and to plan implementation upon receiving an award.

Hand delivery

If you submit your application in paper format by hand delivery, you or a courier service must deliver the original and required copies of your application by hand, on or before the application deadline date, to the exact contact and/or address and within the time and day constraints specified by the funder. For local funders, besides the benefit of saving money on shipping, delivering the proposal yourself will provide added assurance that your application reaches the funder on time.

Mailing or shipping

If you submit your application in paper format by mail through the U.S. Postal Service or a commercial carrier, you must mail the original and required copies of your application on or before the application deadline date. Pay close attention to the deadline; in some cases, the agency will specify the application needs to be *received* by the deadline date; others specify that the application needs to be mailed or *postmarked* by the deadline date. Follow the funder's instructions for labeling the package. There may be one address specified for U.S. Mail and a different address specified for commercial carrier. Ask the counter agent to verify the mailing/shipping label. ALWAYS send your completed application directly from the post office or courier office – do not drop the package in a drop box; you will have no recourse in proving your package was picked up and shipped. Be sure you keep at least one of the following proofs of mailing/shipping:

1. A legibly dated U.S. Postal Service postmark.

2. A legible mail receipt with the date of mailing stamped by the U.S. Postal Service.

3. A dated shipping label, invoice, or receipt from a commercial carrier.

4. Any other proof of mailing acceptable to the funder.

Electronic Submission

There are myriad e-submission systems for transmitting grants: foundation systems, corporate application systems, state government systems, federal government agency systems, Grants.gov, etc. As we have continued to stress, be sure you register well in advance of submission, be familiar with how to navigate through the module(s), and be comfortable with entering and attaching data and understand exactly how to transmit/submit properly.

Grants.gov

To submit your application via Grants.gov, you must complete all steps in the Grants.gov registration process. These steps include: 1) registering your organization or business, a multi-part process that includes registration with the Central Contractor Registry (CCR); 2) registering yourself as an Authorized Organization Representative

(AOR); and 3) getting authorized as an AOR by the authority designated by your agency during the registration process. Details on these steps are outlined in the Grants.gov 3-Step Registration Guide. Please note that the registration process may take five or more business days to complete, and you must have completed all registration steps to allow you to submit successfully an application via Grants.gov. In addition, you will need to update your CCR registration on an annual basis. This may take three or more business days to complete.

Grants.gov can be overwhelming the first few times you use the system for submitting a grant. To ease your use of Grants.gov, we wanted to outline some important submission procedures to ensure your application is received in a timely manner and accepted by the funding agency.

1) Download PureEdge Viewer Software from the Grants.gov web site. This software allows the user to view and modify Grants.gov application kits.

2) You will need the Catalog of Federal Domestic Assistance (CFDA) number or a program announcement number to insure you are taken to the correct funding opportunity on Grants.gov. You can go to the RFP or the Federal Register announcement to obtain the correct CFDA number.

3) On the Grants.gov webpage, select "Download Application."

4) Input program information (CFDA number); Grants.gov will then search its database and bring up the grant application.

5) Provide your e-mail address so Grants.gov can notify you of applications guidelines or application kit changes. For example, you will receive an email if the deadline is extended or addendums are issued with changes to the original RFP or grant.

6) Download the application kit that opens with PureEdge Viewer. You should already have the application guidelines or RFP; however, you can also download them here as well.

7) Open the application kit you downloaded from the Grants.gov website to ascertain what forms are necessary (this changes with each agency and often each opportunity). You should have already familiarized yourself with what forms are required and gathered any data to that is needed to fill them out.

8) Assign a brief file name in first highlighted (yellow) box in the application kit.

9) Save the application kit file to your computer so that you do not lose any data and so that you can work on the application offline and save data on your computer. Please be sure to note where you are saving the Grants.gov file on your computer.

10) Upload the attachments and fill in the required forms. Files must be attached in a .DOC (document), .RTF (rich text), or .PDF (Portable Document) format. If you upload a file type other than the three file types specified in this paragraph or submit a password-protected file, it will not be reviewed. A typical Grants.gov application will consist of:

    a) Standard Form 424 cover sheet and supplemental form

    b) Standard Form 424A or ED 524 (summary budget page)

    c) Various federal certification forms

    d) Project abstract form

    e) Project narrative attachment

    f) Budget narrative attachment

    g) Other attachments (may include resumes, letters of support, research, etc.).

The agency may request that you provide original signatures on forms via fax or at a later date.

11) Once all the final attachments are uploaded and the forms are filled in, review the data for accuracy and to insure all required

items are contained in the kit. Or, ask someone in your office to review the data.

12) If the package is final, save the file again – replace the existing file.

13) Next, click on "check package for errors." If there are errors, the system will notify you one at a time. Keep repeating steps 12 and 13 until the system confirms there are no errors.

14) At this point the "submit" button will be highlighted meaning your application is ready to submit. This step must be completed by the AOR because once the system is done uploading your application it will ask you for your AOR login and password. If you are an AOR for multiple organizations, be sure to use the AOR information that matches the submitting organization's DUNS number.

15) The amount of time it can take to upload an application will vary depending on a variety of factors, including the size of the application and the speed of your Internet connection.

16) A message will be displayed that your application was submitted with the date and time. It will also provide you with a confirmation number – print this page. The agency will not consider your application if it is date and time stamped by the Grants.gov system later than the application deadline date and time. When your application is retrieved by the funder from Grants.gov, they will notify you if they are rejecting your application because it was date and time stamped by the Grants.gov system after the application deadline date and time.

If you experience problems submitting your proposal, contact the Grants.gov Support Desk. Keep a record of the Grants.gov Support Desk Case Number you are assigned. It is possible you can receive an extension, but only for unavailability of, or technical problems with, the Grants.gov system. An extension will not be granted if you failed to fully register before the application deadline date and time or if the technical problem you experienced is unrelated to the Grants.gov system.

Recourse

Confirmed proof that you sent or transmitted your package by the deadline date/time and labeled it as instructed to the exact address specified by the funder and tracking your package verifying it was received and, in some cases, is being reviewed by the funder is responsible recourse. You owe it to yourself to follow this grant through. After all, you put your blood, sweat and tears into all that time planning, preparing, developing and packaging your 'work of art' – not to mention your project needs the money/assistance.

Confirmation

Regardless of submission method, receiving a confirmation gives you a permanent record that your application was postmarked and received within the application deadline by the funder or its designee. This way, if an application is lost in the mail or is trashed by a temporary employee or the delivery guy's dog ate it, you can show proof to the funder that you did everything as required and the agency should grant you permission to send another copy.

Hand delivered

When the application is hand delivered to the agency or funder, be sure to obtain a receipt or confirmation documenting the receipt and acceptance of your grant application. Have the person accepting the application write a date and time on the receipt and either have them sign the receipt or document their name.

Mail or courier

In addition to the proof of mailing you received at the time of sending your package off, you should always confirm the package has been received. If you send your package using the U.S. Postal Service, mail your package 'return receipt' so that you have a signed official document stating the package was received and signed for by the intended recipient. If you send your proposal via courier, be sure to check the box that requires a signature upon delivery and track the package on the Internet using the assigned tracking number. Print the tracking history once the status indicates the package has been delivered and signed for.

Electronic submission

If you submit your application through the Internet via the funder's designated submission site, typically you will receive an automatic acknowledgment when your application is received. Print and file the document for your records. Use the system's tracking features to follow the progress and status of your application. Always print any status changes and keep in your records.

Grants.gov

After you electronically submit your application, Grants.gov will provide an automatic notification of receipt that contains a Grants.gov tracking number. This notification indicates receipt by Grants.gov only, not receipt by the funding agency. The funder will then retrieve your application from Grants.gov and send a second notification to you by e-mail. This second notification indicates that they have received your application and have assigned your application an identifying number unique to your application.

You should also confirm that your submission was on time and successfully received and validated by Grants.gov and the funder. To see the date and time your application was received, log in to Grants.gov and click on the *Track My Application* link. For a successful submission, the date and time received should be earlier than the mandatory deadline date and time.

After you have confirmed your successful submission, you will receive a series of e-mails about the status of your application. Do not rely solely on e-mail to confirm whether your application has been and validated and is being reviewed. As the AOR who submitted the application, you can log in and use the Track My Application feature to follow the proposal through each status: Validated, Received by Agency, or Agency Tracking Number Assigned. Once the application status reaches Agency Tracking Number Assigned, it is in the funder's hands. Be sure to document the tracking number for your records.

If your application has a status of "Rejected with Errors," your application has not been received successfully. For detailed reasons why your application may be rejected, review the Grants.gov *Application Error Tips* document found on their website. You usually can correct the errors and resubmit. You can also contact the support desk for assistance.

Tracking systems

It is extremely important that you track all your submissions. Make a file for each funder and store contact information, proposals and attachments. Save proposals electronically to your computer and keep a final hard-copy on file so you can quickly retrieve the information. Develop a grant application database with key information similar to the following sample:

Funder	Project Desc.	$ Req.	Deadline	Submitted	Date confirmed and method	Follow-up Date & Contact	Final Status-Date-Contact-Amount (if award)
Grant Title: Safe Schools Healthy Students Program							
DOE							
Grant Title: ABC Foundation Excitement for Education Grant							
ABC Fdn.							
Grant Title:							
Grant Title:							

Successful submission

Aaah… sweet success! You have confirmed the application is being reviewed by the funder. Good luck!

Chapter 6

Your Grant Has Been Submitted

What Do You Do Now?

Well, you have your life back. Now what are you going to do? You have probably been going non-stop for weeks, but now that your proposal is in the hands of the funder you are wondering what is next. This is the part that gets a little difficult...sorry fellow control freaks, what happens next is not in your control. You can, however, understand the post submission process and know what your role is during the review process and after a decision is made.

Follow-up after submission

There are three types of follow-up: 1) initiating contact with the funder directly by email or telephone; 2) receiving a notice from the funder that your application/proposal has been received and in some cases, what the next steps will be; and 3) receiving a request from the funder for additional information or requesting a visit to your site

Contacting the funder

Unless the funder requests that you do not contact them after submission, contacting the funder to follow-up is a positive action that further cultivates a relationship with the funder. Following up shows the funder that you really want to be funded, demonstrates good communication and also reinforces the importance of their participation in your program/project. The more you work with the same funders, the better acquainted you will become with their preferred methods of communication. Do not be discouraged if the funder does not respond to your call or keeps the contact extremely brief. Chances are they are swamped. Aren't we all!

A good strategy our staff follows or recommends to our clients to initiate contact with the funder includes these steps:

1. Determine who will be the representative to have contact with the funder. This person should be the primary contact. Be consistent; do not confuse things by having multiple staff calling the funder. It may be the authorized representative (Executive Director, Superintendent, CEO, etc.); it may be the

project director, or if your grant writing role is more of a fundraiser position, it could be you.

2. After you have mailed your application, have the representative call or email the funder to let them know you have applied. Just a brief call or note is fine, noting that your application was mailed and will be received by the due date and that you are looking forward to hearing from them soon.

3. Before any further follow-up is made, the representative should reread the proposal and make sure they are comfortable and familiar with its content.

4. Approximately two weeks after you confirm the funder has received your proposal, call or email again. If you sent a cover letter with your proposal package and promised a follow-up in your closing, follow-up accordingly. This shows you keep your word and are organized.

5. When calling or emailing the funder, let them know you are just following up on your submission and ask them if they have any further questions.

6. If your representative has re-read the proposal, the information should be fresh in his/her mind, have a copy of the proposal open for quick reference just to ensure the representative can answer any questions the funder may have.

7. If the funder seems welcoming, provide any accomplishments or progress on the project since submittal. Include any other awards or denials you may have received from other funders that you mentioned in your proposal/letter that you were soliciting. Do not get off track or babble on; just contribute brief information on anything that can add support to your project.

8. Also, take this opportunity to find out the funder's next steps. When do they expect to announce awards or make a decision? How will they contact you?

9. Thank them for their time. Always be polite, brief, enthusiastic and genuine.

Acknowledgement from the funder

Several funder agencies will send out postcards or form letters stating that they have received your proposal and it is being reviewed. Other agencies rely on the automated response from your electronic application to acknowledge your application. The acknowledgement might include how they prefer to be contacted and what the next step of the process is. An acknowledgement form letter might look something like this:

Dear Applicant:

I am writing simply to inform you that your proposal dated **Month 00, 20__**, has been received at the Foundation and is under review.

We will get back to you in about six weeks with the results of our review.

Cordially,

Staff Name

Title

Track the notification and any upcoming dates in your grant tracking system and file the original for your records.

Additional information requests

The funder may email or call you with a request for additional information. Be sure that the personal named as the primary contact for the grant is constantly monitoring their email, mail and voicemail after submission. Typically a request for additional information is a good sign that you have made it through the initial review process but, this does not guarantee you are going to be awarded the grant. An additional request may be a simple request or may be a request for signature pages or it may be a detailed list of questions. Roll with the punches! Get them what they want as quickly as you can. And yes, as you've probably anticipated, we advise you to follow their instructions exactly.

Even if the funder gives you a quick turnaround time for responding to their request for additional information, do not, DO NOT, turn the response in after their deadline. If you are unable to answer the questions in the time allotted, or the person who received the request was out on vacation, contact the funder immediately and discuss an extension. You do not want to throw something together which would negatively impact your application. Not responding at all would basically eliminate your chances for funding.

A request might look something like the following sample.

Dear Mr. Smith,

The Office of Safe and Drug-Free Schools is conducting a routine, preliminary review of applications submitted for the FY 2007 XYZ discretionary grant competition.

Before we can further consider the application submitted by **ABC School District (PR/Award Number XXXXX)**, we need you to please provide the following information:

1) Please complete the Grants.gov Lobbying Form. This form must be signed by the Authorized Representative for the district and faxed to me at 555-555-5555 or emailed as .pdf documents to me at XXX.

2) The 524 Form and the budget narrative explain that the district has an approved indirect cost rate of X%. Please provide proof that this is the approved rate for your district.

If you have any questions about the preceding requests, please do not hesitate to contact me at (555) 555-5555. **If not, please provide all of the requested information to my attention via fax (555-555-555) or email (<u>xxx</u>) no later than 5 pm ET on Tuesday, Month/Day, 2007 to be further considered under this competition. <u>PLEASE be sure to include your project's Tracking number on all pages of all documents and communications sent in response to this email.</u>**

Thank you, in advance, for your timely response to this request,

Ms. Doe

Site visit requests

And you dreaded the in-laws' visits? Site visits will be nerve racking, but a very good sign and should be looked at positively. Think of it this way. Would you send two staff members on a paid trip to interview a potential job candidate if you weren't seriously interested? This meeting can be a great way to get to know your potential funding partner and get a feel for how interested they are in your program.

Site visits are very important to most funders. An excellent proposal does not mean the organization/individual can really manage a grant. The purpose of the site visit is to get to know your leadership and staff, discuss the project with the project planning team and key project personnel and have the person who manages finances answer any of their budget questions.

When the funder calls to schedule a site visit, find out: who, what and when. Who will be coming – names and titles? Who do they want to meet with? What will the agenda be – what does the funder want to see? When will they be at your site and for how long? You should prepare for your site visit based on the answers to these questions. Use common sense; do not order new furniture or roll out a red carpet. Prepare for their visit by making sure your team is well versed on what the program is about, what everyone's roles are and how you plan to keep the program operating after the grant ends.

Although additional information and site visit requests are not assurances that your grant will be funded, it does mean that your program/project fits a funder's priorities and is being seriously considered for funding.

Award announcement process

Each grantmaker has its own application review process. During the review process the funder will usually use a ranking system and final judgment process for each applicant's proposal. This multi-step process yields who the funder will award grants to. At this point you will be notified of the status of your application which will be either funded, not-funded or placed on hold.

What is involved in the ranking process?

Step 1 - Each funder will use a panel of reviewers to evaluate your proposal. The panel can be a selection of peer reviewers. Reviewers score each application against the selection criteria published in the guidelines or RFP.

Step 2 – After the application is reviewed, the panel scores are used to develop a rank order list. The panel score is derived from averaging or normalizing the scores from each reviewer on the panel that reviewed a particular application. In some cases, more common for government grants, normalizing is done through a computer program which will compensate for the tendencies of some reviewers to score applications higher or lower than other reviewers for the same group of applications. With normalized scores, the grant teams are able to prepare a rank order list of applications that negates, as much as feasible, any unusual variations in scoring.

Step 3 – A cut-off point is established for the rank order list based on the availability of support for the program.

Step 4 – A cost analysis is performed on those applications that scored high enough on the list to be considered for funding. The cost analysis is performed to determine whether the proposed costs of an applicant's budget are allowable, allocable, and reasonable. The funder's giving director or government program staff (grant team) will review the narrative and budget of applications being considered for funding to ensure the costs directly relate to the activities and objectives of the project. All unallowable costs are deleted from the budget.

Step 5 – The grant team notes any concerns or questions about the application or the budget and contacts the applicant to get more detailed information before a funding decision is made.

Step 6 – Once any questions are answered, a formal list is developed of the applicants who are being recommended for funding. The list will also include the recommended funding levels.

Step 7 – The list is reviewed by the funder's leadership for final approval. In some cases the grant team may even be authorized to approve the list. Even if your proposal ranks high and the grant team considers it for funding, your application still might not be funded because of one or more of the following reasons: the large number of high quality applications that were received for the competition; there are limited funds available for the program; and/or there is a geographic distribution requirement for the number of grants awarded to specific regions of the country for the program.

Step 8 – Once the list is approved by leadership, the grant team notifies applicants of their status.

Notification

You may receive funding or a hold notification in several ways: letter, phone call, email, or a federal government Grant Award Notification (GAN). Typically if you are not funded, you will receive a standard rejection letter.

The most common formal award notification is a letter. A standard letter might look something like this:

Month 00, 20__

Contact Person

Title

Organization/individual

Street Address

City, State

Dear _____:

I am pleased to tell you that a grant to **GRANTEE ORGANIZATION/INDIVIDUAL'S LEGAL NAME** in the amount of $**AMOUNT OF GRANT** has been approved to support **PROJECT TITLE**. In order to receive your check—which will be mailed to you in early **MONTH**—we ask that you send back to us a countersigned copy of this letter.

Please note that these grant funds must be used substantially in accordance with the budget included with your proposal and that no substantial changes in the budget or the grant period may be made without prior written approval from the Foundation. Any funds not used for the purposes described in this letter will revert to the Foundation.

A condition of this grant is that you agree to submit fiscal and narrative reports on or about **Month 00, 20__**. This grant is subject to financial audit upon our notification during or immediately following the grant period. A separate bank account for the grant is not required, but it is necessary that a separate accounting of this grant be maintained.

We request that in any publicity given this grant, acknowledgment be made that funds were received from the Foundation. Please enclose copies of any publicity when you send us your report.

Sincerely yours,

Staff Name

Title

Accepted by:

_____

           Name, Title   Date

Some agencies or funders may call you prior to sending you the award letter to congratulate you personally. In some cases, you will be notified of a federal grant award by receiving an official Grant Award Notification (GAN) through the mail without any prior contact from the agency. The GAN is the official document that states the terms, conditions, and amount of an award. The GAN letter will also include attachments which spell out additional terms and conditions of the award and enclosures that give further guidance on administrative procedures. The attachments and enclosures contain important information about your award and you are urged to pay particular attention to them as you read the GAN. Two copies of the GAN are mailed to each grantee: 1) the authorized representative and 2) the project director.

Federal government grant making agencies may also send notification letters to members of Congress from states where applicants being considered for funding are located. As a result, applicants sometimes receive news of the status of their application from their congressional delegations as well.

A funder may want to make a conditional offer. If the grantmaker is requesting a significant change to a proposal, a grant team member may contact you to make a funding offer before making a grant award. You have the choice to either accept or reject the changes and funding offer.

It is possible you ranked slightly below the funded group. In this case you may receive a letter advising that you are in a 'hold' funding status. While being funded is not guaranteed, having ranked slightly lower than the funded group, you still have a chance of being funded if additional funds become available or if one or more of the funded applicants declines an offer of award.

Your grant was funded – what now?

The big day has finally arrived. The funder notifies you by letter, phone, or e-mail that your application has been funded. What? Really? Excitement sets in. You breathe a sigh of relief and then ask..."What now?" One could say that the real work begins at this point. There will be post-award communications and discussions with the funder, maybe even face-to-face visits; the beginning of a partnership between you and the funder. You will deal with alerting the media and informing project partners. And then, of course, you will implement your project, which will go on for a year or more.

It is always a nice touch to send a hand-written thank you note or, if the funder is local, stop in to say thank you. Funders appreciate genuine expressions of gratitude.

Post award communication

The partnership process focuses on establishing and cultivating relationships to promote and ensure successful project outcomes. Frequent and on-going communications will be instrumental throughout the life of the project. In most cases a specific contact will be assigned to your project by the funder. We encourage grantees to use the funder as a resource in attaining their project's goals.

Post award communication can be a face-to-face meeting, telephone discussion, workshop, notes sent via fax or mail, via email or a combination of a variety of methods. Initial communication will take place shortly after a new grant is awarded, but usually not later than 90 days after the award date. This is also the time the funder will clarify record management and monitoring practices.

Grantees are urged to communicate with their assigned contact at the funder agency as often as necessary to ensure that substantial progress is made during the funding period. This person is assigned to you to stand ready to answer questions, provide technical assistance, and help you better understand requirements and procedures to ensure that you achieve the goals of your project. They want you to succeed!

Contract

Most grant makers will require that you sign a letter of agreement or some other form of contract upon award to commit to carry out your project in a way that is consistent with the requirements of the RFP/grant guidelines. This begins before you even receive an award notification; it begins with the application process. You should make yourself very familiar with the program regulations when you are filling out the required forms and preparing your application for submission. Your agreement will outline the details of the grant and reporting expectations.

Reporting Requirements

Finishing project activities by the end of a budget or project period is only half the story of a grant project. The other half is telling the funder about it. You should put as much care into timely, accurate, and comprehensive reporting of your project components as you put into planning those same activities during the writing and development process. Your reporting, in turn, becomes the basis for the funder's evaluation of the effectiveness of its programs, as well as its own reporting to its leadership and/or board of directors. Additionally, renewals of multi-year awards are reliant on the project making satisfactory progress in meeting objectives.

Most funders will expect you to submit a final performance report, including financial information, at the end of your project period. Not sending reports or other required documents can place you in noncompliance with the terms and conditions of the grant award or agreement. Noncompliance jeopardizes your chance for future funding from the funder. Therefore, it is critical that you send all your reports by the due dates. Reporting requirements, forms and deadlines will be conveyed to you during post award communication.

Record Management

The receipt of a grant carries the obligation to maintain comprehensive, appropriate, accurate, and complete records of all program operations and fiscal transactions. Any document requiring a signature must be executed by the authorized representative. It is essential to establish an organized records management system for your grant project. A funder may request to examine and audit your records at any time. Grant records must be retained for a period of at least three years or the time period defined by your agreement/contract.

Notifying project partners

When you have been notified of your grant award, you should share the good news with any project partners. After all, your project was funded based, in part, on the strengths that your partners bring to the table. It is a good idea to contact them before they read it in a press release; this will start the relationship off on a good note. Calling is always the most personable method, especially since you will be working with them for at least a year. You want to convey your enthusiasm. Be sure to set a tentative call or meeting date to go over grant and award details. A letter or an email can also be used to communicate the award, next steps and a time/date for a meeting or a call.

Media

Being awarded a grant is a huge accomplishment and should be publicized. A public announcement through media and other community groups will share your success as well as recognize the funder. When the news gets out about your grant award, everyone wins. You receive positive attention for the important work you are doing, which can spark the interest of other funders. The funder and its donors are recognized, promoting more investment in community projects and support for future donor receipts.

- ♣ Publicize grants by sending press releases to local media and by featuring articles in your own publications, on your website and at your board meetings or community events. Some ideas and tips on publicizing a grant award:

- ♣ Include news of your grant in any publications you produce for internal or external distribution, such as newsletters, brochures, annual reports, lists of supporters, board minutes, etc.

- ♣ Contact local media, including weekly community newspapers and special interest publications, using either a news release or via a personal phone call. Add appropriate quotes and contact information from key people in your organization/business. If you want to include photos, submit one or two carefully chosen photographs that show off your grant project. Be sure that you have permission from the subjects to use these images.

- Invite the press to a grand opening ceremony, check presentation ceremony or other event associated with the project.

- Include the funder's name and logo on signs, plaques or program materials that recognize donors at your events or facilities or on publicity material related to your program.

- Provide a link to the funder's website on your web site.

- Contact your funder for suggestions on appropriate media outlets and contacts, a quick review of your press release or general brainstorming on possibilities for publicity.

- Even after the award period is over, report positive news about the impact of this grant to local media.

Your funder may provide you with a press release template. We have also provided samples below for you

Press Release Template

Date

(Funder Name) Grant to Encourage Greater Community Use of XYZ Center

The XYZ Community Center has been awarded a (Funder Name) grant of $(amount) towards the cost of computers and outdoor play equipment.

The XYZ Community Center is a 'not-for-profit' community organization that offers a broad range of services to the XYZ community, including child care, playgroups, migrant English classes, beginner computer courses, and craft and hobby courses.

XYZ Community Center Chairperson, (Chairperson Name) said that the grant for computers would enable many more members of the community to learn basic computer skills.

'At the moment we only have four computers and so only a few people can attend each course', she said.

'The new computers will give lots more people the opportunity to attend these popular courses.'

The grant for outdoor play equipment will be used by the six different playgroups - including a new group specifically for English language learners - that use the Center.

The (Funder Name) Grant will be presented to the XYX Community Center by the Member for XYZ, (Member Name) during a special open day at the Center.	
Date:	Tuesday, Month Day, Year
Time:	9.30 am - 12.00 noon (10.00 am for check presentation)
Venue:	XYZ Community Center Community Street, XYZ

The local community will be invited to visit the Center for the check presentation. There will be a barbeque and activities for children.

Photo ideas: Children using the new play equipment;
Our oldest participant is 80-year-old, who is doing a computer course so she can receive emails from her family overseas. (Name) could be photographed at a computer or at the play equipment with some of the children.

For further information please contact: (Chairperson Name), Chairperson XYZ Community Center on 555-555-555 or ABC@xyz.com

Funder provided template sample

SAMPLE PRESS RELEASE ANNOUNCING A CONGRESSIONALLY-DIRECTED GRANT

Please include reference to "*a Congressionally-directed grant through the Department of Education*" as your funding source in all press releases, in all publications, and on any Web sites related to the project.

Work with your institution's public relations staff to send out information on your project to local print and news media. Your institution may have its own template for creating the press release; but below is a sample format you may use for issuing a press release for the grant award.

SAMPLE PRESS RELEASE FORMAT

Contact: Project Director's Name, Address, Phone Number, E-mail Address

For Immediate Release

Date:

****MEDIA ALERT****

Congress Awards Grant to *Name of Institution*

For *Name of Project*

WHAT: The U.S. Congress, through the Department of Education, has awarded a *amount of the award* grant to the *name of the institution and department* for the *name of the project*. *Name the percentage of federal funds used for the project, e.g., sixty percent* of this *name the total cost of the*

> *project, e.g., two million dollar project* is funded by
> federal government, with the remaining *name the*
> *percentage* funded by *non-governmental sources.*

WHEN: The *name of the project* activities begin *date* and extend to
end date.

DETAILS: *Description of the project. Abstract used for submission*
would be appropriate.

Publicity can work both ways. Do not be surprised if the media contacts you first. Award announcements are often published on websites or through government agency press releases. If you have a public information officer or communications person on staff, this person should handle or assist you with any media contact or publicity campaign. If you do not have a staff member who handles publicity, discuss your strategy with your staff or board of directors prior to initiating contact or answering any questions. Publicity efforts can backfire if they aren't done right or if the wrong information is published. Be sure the project details are correct and the funder's information is accurate and spelled correctly.

Media portfolio

It is a good idea to keep a portfolio of all publicity, even internal materials. In addition to filing media materials you can also forward copies of any clippings of articles or information about coverage in broadcast media to your assigned funder contact. Your portfolio can be used to support your future fundraising and is a good way to report positive progress to your funder. As a grant writer, your portfolio will demonstrate your successful track record.

Your grant was not funded – what now?

Funders will inform you if your application is not evaluated or selected for funding. A proposal rejection is not the end of the world.

Seek your reviewers' comments by calling or emailing the funder. Some funders may even automatically mail you your reviewer scores and comments. Reviewer's comments can be used to strengthen areas that the reviewer noted as weak, so that you can resubmit a stronger proposal for the next funding cycle.

Talking with funders or using reviewer comments to understand why your proposal wasn't funded may not always be an option. If not, here is a list of reasons why a proposal may not be funded:

- The funder is over committed to funding other organizations/individuals or has limited resources.

- There is already a similar project in your geographic area or an application that ranks higher than yours in a neighboring city.

- The agency decides to fund applicants that ranked high in a previous competition.

- Your application ranked high, but others ranked higher.

- There were bonus points that placed other applications above yours.

- The funder experienced a budget shortfall.

- Idea is just too new and innovative.

- Political reasons

- Proposal is poorly written or is hard to understand.

- Precise instructions were not followed.

- Application exceeded the specified page limit(s). Consult the grantor agency if instructions do not specify whether page limits include resumes, attachments, etc., or if they are in addition to such items.

- Proposal lacks evidence of coordination with other individuals and organizations working in the same area.

- Program objectives do not match the objectives of the funder.

- Proposal contains too many footnotes and references citing authorities, which conveys a lack of original thinking.

- Proposal rambles and is unclear, reflecting a plan that is poorly devised and hastily thought out.

- Needs were not adequately defined.

- Project components are weakly stated, vague, or too general.

- Budget does not relate to the proposed objectives and activities; budgeted items are not sufficiently justified as necessary and reasonable for accomplishing the objectives; budget does not reflect adequate planning to accomplish the proposed objectives and activities.

- Budget contains non-allowable expenses.

- Evidence of capability to successfully manage the proposed project is insufficient or absent.

- Evaluation procedures are inadequate and poorly constructed.

- Proposal was not mailed or delivered by the specified deadline date.

- Proposal was not mailed using an acceptable proof of mailing.

We truly hope that you receive more award notices than rejection letters in your grant writing efforts. Win or lose, you are networking! Many grant applications are reviewed by a panel of your peers so grant writing is a great way to get your name out, expose your peers to your work, and start to build your contacts. Feel good about any awards you receive, you deserve it! Consider the grants that you do not receive as valuable practice and learn from the experience. In our experience, we've had repeated success with clients that do not receive funding for a highly-competitive proposal the first time, but after strengthening the proposal using reviewer's comments, it is fully funded the second time around.

Chapter 7

**To Hire a Professional Grant Writer or
Not to Hire a Professional Grant Writer?**

Working with a professional grant writer – whether you hire a staff writer or contract with a professional on a freelance basis -- can be a great solution IF you have the time to commit to work with the professional. The professional grant writer's job is to assist you with your grant proposal – but it is your vision and project design. Organizations/individuals that see the success or failure of securing grants as the sole responsibility of the grant writer are failing to consider something even more important than the grant application -- the funding goals. Poorly delineated projects, ambiguous budgets, inexperienced project personnel and a host of other weaknesses cannot be overcome by a well-crafted grant proposal. Although form and properly following guidelines are critical to being funded, the awarding of grants has more to do with function and grant writers are not usually the ones who make the policy and practice recommendations that initiate grant seeking and fundraising.

Benefits of Hiring a Professional Grant Writer

Preparing grants requires time and skill. Even with a comprehensive written guide and the wealth of information available on the Internet, the process can be complex at best. Hiring a professional grant writer can help you realize your funding goals more quickly, as well as the obvious – it frees up your time from having to write a proposal when you have a million other professional responsibilities. A professional grant writer can walk you through the process, identify potential funding sources, narrow those sources down and then write the letter of inquiry and/or a full proposal for you. Voila! You look brilliant and you have not missed a night's sleep!

Grant writer services are not cheap however, so weigh the cost of hiring a professional versus the benefit – is a commitment of $2,500 for a proposal to be written a good investment on the potential to receive a $100,000 grant award? While there is no guarantee that you will be funded for every application you submit, a professional grant writer with a proven track record of funding awards is definitely going to increase your odds of receiving an award.

A less obvious benefit to working with a professional is that you will have access to their wealth of experience and knowledge in the grant writing and fundraising world. At our company, our team's approach to providing professional services is comprehensive. We work closely with our clients from program design through the finished application, handle the submission and track the progress for you. We focus on establishing long-term relationships with clients, which requires more than just providing the actual writing of the proposal to extend to a variety of support services. To maximize the services you have access to when hiring a professional grant writer, look for someone that provides some of the following:

Support Services

- ♣ Customized funding plan development

- ♣ Best-practice program research that matches a particular project

- ♣ Grant planning worksheets and templates to help navigate the writing process

- ♣ Information display templates that effectively communicate required information in the allotted space

- ♣ Editorial and criteria reviews of proposals written by your organization

For example, Grant Writers Institute LLC offers cost-effective solutions for organizations/individuals that do not have the funds to create and maintain their own in-house grants office/department. They offer custom subscription services – individual or in a package – designed to fully support individuals, non-profits and organization/individuals in securing additional revenue streams for special projects, etc. and it is all done virtually. They offer customized research and funding searches, customized comprehensive funding alert emails, development of a complete virtual grants office fully supported by experience professionals and a variety of other services. (www.grantwritersinstitute.org.)

Selecting a Grant Writer

It may be that grant writing just is not your cup of tea and everyone else in your organization or company is either wearing too many hats already, or the word "grants" sends them screaming out of the room. Where do you find a professional, qualified grant writer?

Methods to recruit grant writer candidates

There are several resources available to you in seeking an independent consultant or a staff grant writer. Recommendations, Internet postings, news articles, professional associations, etc. are the most widely used methods for hiring or retaining a grant writer.

Word of mouth is by far the most fool-proof way to find an effective and experienced candidate. Professionals recommended by colleagues and your peers have demonstrated their abilities and talent. Call a variety of colleagues and inquire about any grant writers they might have hired on a consulting basis. Searching online job or freelance postings will require more effort from your part. Posting an ad for a grant writer will return a potpourri of applicants. You will review resumes, hold interviews and then make a selection. Some sites are free, but other carry a cost for posting. You will also need to dedicate the time to review, interview and select your grant writer.

Press releases often publish information on different individual or organizational successes in securing grants. Look in your local newspaper archives online. If the article mentions a grant writer, contact that writer yourself to determine if they would be a possible fit for your grant writing needs. Or call the organization or individual, and see if they will make a recommendation for a writer they've had success with.

Another option is to contact the nearest chapter of the Association of Fundraising Professionals (AFP) in your area to search for a grant writer. They provide a directory of nearly 28,000 members and professionals in more than 190 chapters throughout the world. Additionally, they have a job center that matches members/professionals and employers through job postings and a database of fundraising

117

professionals' resumes. The association's purpose is to foster development and growth of fundraising professionals and promotes high ethical standards in the fundraising profession.

Local grant writer vs. remote grant writer

Keep an open mind when searching for a professional grant writer. Although you may find a great candidate right in your own community that can work with you on-site at your agency, there are a growing number of professionals that work successfully with clients remotely. Our team works from their offices across the country – location is not an obstacle with today's technology. Communication and document sharing by phone, fax and email have paved the way to successful professional relationships that know no geographic boundaries.

Selecting a writer

The growing need for financial assistance coupled with the mystery that seems to surround successful grant writing creates a large demand for accomplished, experienced grant writing consultants. But how do you determine whether they possess those qualities? Whether you have received the consultants name through a recommendation or the person is answering your job posting, it is important you do your research as well as interview the candidate in person or over the phone. Your selection is important. You most likely wouldn't buy a car or a house out of the classifieds sites unseen. If your neighbor recommended a babysitter, you probably wouldn't leave your children with him/her without an interview.

Research

Thank goodness for Google and other search engines! As you receive names of potential candidates, get on the Internet. Do a general search. Search with quotes "Joe Schmo" or "Joe Schmo" + grants. If there are several articles or board minutes with positive mention of this person – good deal. If there is no mention of this person – good deal, but do further research. If your search provides you with some real "whoppers" – steer clear.

Other practical research is to ask the consultant to provide references and writing samples, both funded and non-funded. Call the references and speak with the contact listed and possibly another individual within the company to inquire about the person's performance, work ethic and personality. Ask if they were happy with the results. Did they feel as though they were included in the process? Did the writer work well with the staff? Were they interested in learning about the organization or individual's business? Samples of funded and non-funded grants are a great way to evaluate and measure the quality of a grant writer's work. Funded proposals demonstrate a successful track record as well as organization, delivery, writing style, etc. Proposals that were not funded can provide assurance that the proposal was still executed properly, organized, and sold the program/project well vs. a proposal that wasn't funded due to sloppiness and poor delivery.

Interviews

You may decide to interview if the consultant passes the background phase. The interview process is really your time to "click" with the candidate. Remember, they are interviewing you too. Some people will know right away if they will be able to work with the writer, or it may be further in the discussion when the individuals are able to warm-up. Do not rely on "clicking" alone. Many people are extremely professional and will maintain this composure at all times. Ask your interviewee questions and chat about their experience. Here are some good discussion points:

- ♣ Number and type of proposals they have written.

- ♣ Reputation.

- ♣ Experience with funders.

- ♣ Discuss their sample proposals.

- ♣ Ask if they are also writing for other clients (you may or may not care).

119

♣ Ask about pricing/cost, but do not rush to make price *the* deciding factor

♣ Ask the professional what types of grants they have experience in? Do they have experience and success in winning grants for your type of agency and needs? A well-rounded professional should be able to acclimate to any topic or field.

Qualities to look for in choosing a professional grant writer

A professional grant writer not only needs to be able to write a grant - but also have the desire to get it funded. There are a number of characteristics and qualities to take into account when looking to hire a professional grant writer.

♣ Excellent communication and writing skills

♣ Keen knowledge of grant sources and research skills

♣ Very organized

♣ Detail oriented

♣ Disciplined work ethic – able to work efficiently and independently

♣ Effective at meeting deadlines

♣ Flexibility

♣ Able to prioritize multiple projects and tasks

♣ Creativity

♣ Resourceful

Ask the writer how they manage a project to ensure that they keep the project on time. Check references to see if their current or previous clients can speak to their 'customer service' skills, ability to communicate clearly during the process, and how they might have handled multiple projects. The purpose of hiring a professional is to make your job easier. You should expect that the person you hire will:

♣ Establish a timeline for your completing the project to ensure that the project stays on track, meets with the client's work schedule and allows sufficient time to provide information client information and documents and review the draft narratives

♣ Schedule and prepare an agenda for a telephone design meeting to ask cogent questions and determine a single point of contact for additional information.

♣ Prepare draft letters of support, Memorandum of Understanding/Agreement and other documents as appropriate for the agency's approval.

♣ Finalize Online or mail submission to the funder

Red Flags

There are a few things that you will want to be alert to as you go through the process of selecting and hiring a grant writer. If the professional guarantees that you will receive every grant that you apply for, do not fall for it. Grant writers touting guarantees to impress potential employers or to seal the deal are taking advantage of your inexperience regarding grant writing. Grant writing is a competitive process, so unless funding is a sure bet (e.g., based on formula/entitlement), always assume demand is higher than supply and there are no guarantees.

Compensation

Compensation for a professional grant writer varies depending on the geographic location, the professional's experience and type of service offered. A true professional will work with your budget within reason, but the pricing structure can be established in a variety of ways. The costs below are just estimates, keeping in mind that there are many areas of the country where the market will bear higher rates.

♣ Per narrative page pricing ranges from $25 - $200, depending on the grant writer's experience and proven ability.

♣ By the project – a flat fee rate for completing the entire grant proposal (the cost should include submission). The standard per-project rates vary across professionals, but a seasoned professional with a proven track record of grant awards for their clients and a solid reputation for reliability and customer service will usually compute this pricing based on the higher end of a per-page rate. So for example, a 25-page narrative project might be priced between $2,500 and $5,000 per proposal. Keep in mind the complexity of your project; this factor will greatly impact the pricing.

♣ Retainer pay is a set monthly fee for a pre-determined amount of work for usually a one-year period. This method is usually considered for long term projects, offering a discount for a guaranteed quantity of work for a set time period. This is often an attractive option if you have developed a pretty extensive Funding Strategy, because knowing the total grant writer expenses for the year can help you budget and plan for the expense.

♣ An hourly rate for work is usually a better financial option for grant writer services such as grant research or developing your funding goals and funding strategy, rather than actual grant writing. To pay a grant writer on an hourly basis can be more costly because the time it takes to complete a grant can vary greatly depending on the scope of the project and how efficiently the writer is able to complete the project. You can expect to pay an average of $40-60 per hour, with slightly higher hourly rates for writers in large, major cities.

♣ Contingent pay, or paying a grant writer a percentage of the total grant funds awarded has become a common practice. This is your choice of course, but our company's personal philosophy on this payment method is that grant writers are performing a professional service and should be compensated upon completing the project. More importantly, the funds received from a grant award are for specific expenses in your project. Some grants allow you to write the costs of your grant writer into the budget. If your grant writer agrees to this, they are agreeing to not being paid until the grant is awarded. If the grant is not funded, a contingency for payment needs to be worked out between you and the writer.

The agency's role in working with a professional grant writer.

While you want a professional grant writer that will take you from planning your proposal contents to writing and finally submitting your

application, you can expect that you will be required to be fully engaged in the process. The writer may ask for information that already exists at your agency. Because you are on top of your game, you have already gathered some of this important information that we discussed in Chapter 3.

- ♣ Copies of plans, proposals or other information that is already inexistence and were mentioned in your program design call

- ♣ Numbers and data such as staff salaries, fringe benefit costs, indirect cost information, numbers of clients to be served, budget information for particular purchases, etc.

- ♣ Short, factual items or key program decisions (i.e. partnering agencies) on which to base pieces of the narrative

- ♣ Agency-specific information such as DUNS number, EIN, etc.

♣ Evaluation reports from other funded projects

On the agency side, the grant writer will need you to attend a telephone or in-person design meeting where you review the key elements of the grant. You should also be accessible by telephone throughout the process to field questions as needed. Your help in securing signatures for forms or letters will also be required. Most grant writers will provide up to 2 draft responses to the proposal for the client's review. Take the time to review the draft and give feedback and answer any questions for missing information during the draft process. The grant writer will also need you to thoroughly read and approve the final application.

Conclusion

Grant seeking and grant writing are time-consuming endeavors that require concentrated effort, commitment and persistence. Whether you are just starting out or you are brushing up on your skills, please keep in mind that "people" are making the funding decisions for your application. Whether it is a federal staff, a corporate group or a non-profit foundation board, choosing to fund projects is a difficult decision for the people at the table. There are almost always more applications than money available, so making your application stand out, and double-checking to be sure your project fits the funder's criteria are the best ways to increase your funding odds. Remember that no matter how great a foundation's assets, there are limitations in terms of what they can achieve. We would like to believe that in the ideal world, granters would fund our programs because we've written a great proposal and we really need the funding. But the reality is that the individuals who apply the policies and the funding criteria to our grant applications come to the decision-making table with individual views and opinions.

Granting agencies are shaped by individual board members and staff who often do not live and work in your community, so it is your job to tell them who you are and what your community is like. The business of giving is personal and experiential (within the confines of guidelines and criteria). The funding bottom line boils down to the people at the table, the money available and how well you communicate your message.

Just like a RFP or a grant guidance, I know this book has bombarded you with a tremendous amount of information. If you approach the steps in this guide the same way you approach preparing for and writing a grant proposal, one step at a time, it will soon become second nature to you and you will be writing and submitting grants on your own in no time. If you truly do not have time to write your own grant proposal and decide to work with a professional, this guide can certainly prepare you to understand your grant writer's 'grant speak,' as well as be prepared for your role in the process. Keep your funding goals and priorities

in sight to keep you motivated and remember, if you want to win the lottery, you have to buy a ticket!

Lever, Rob. "US Charitable Giving Sets New Record Topping Katrina Effort." Washington (Agence France-Presse). 25 June 2007. The Raw Story. 17 September 2007.

Poderis, Tony. "Positioning Grant Writers For Success." Fund-raising Forum. April, 2002. 20 September 2007.

U.S. Department of Education. "What Should I Know About ED Grants?" US Department of Education Grants. September 1998. 17 September 2007.

National Council for Voluntary Organizations. "Fundraising Strategy Essentials." National Council for Voluntary Orginisations. 2005-2007. 12 September 2007.

Lotterywest Foundation. "Acknowledging Your Grant - Sample Media Release." Lotterywest Grants. 1 March 2005. 21 September 2007.

Academic Improvement and Teacher Quality Programs. "Improving Literacy Through School Libraries." U.S. Department of Education Grants. 24 September 2007.

Dollar General Corporation. "Youth Literacy Grants." Dollar General Grant Programs. 2007. 24 September 2007.

General Services Administration, Office of Chief Acquisition Officer, Regulatory and Federal Assistance Division (VIR). "Developing and Writing Grant Proposals." The Catalog of Federal Domestic Assistance. 2007. 24 September 2007.

Office of Impact Aid. "Impact aid Section 8007b Discretionary Construction Grant Program." U.S. Department of Education Grants. 2007. 24 September 2007.

Office of Postsecondary Education – Congressionally-Directed Grants. "Sample Press Release Announcing a Congressionally-Directed Grant." US Department of Education. 2005. 21 September 2007.

Toyota Motor Sales. "Toyota Family Literacy Initiative." Toyota About Us. 2003. 24 September 2007.

U.S. Department of Education Office of Safe and Drug-Free Schools. Readiness and Emergency Management for Schools Information and Application Procedures for Fiscal Year 2007. U.S. Department of Education, 2007

U.S. Department of Health and Human Services. "About Grants.gov."
Grants.gov. 2007. 18 September 2007.

The Grantsmanship Center, 1998. Consulting Fees for Grant Proposal Writing:
An Exchange of Ideas and Information from TGCI-Forum.

Grant Writers Institute

For help in finding, writing and developing a grant proposal contact

Grant Writers Institute.

To apply

For one-on-one help from Lynne Paeno and her team of writers

Call 1-877-296-9387 or www.grantwritersinstititue.org